· THE ·
HUNGRY TRAVELER
ITALY

· THE ·
HUNGRY TRAVELER
ITALY

·::·

Pat Mozersky

**Andrews McMeel
Publishing**
Kansas City

ISBN: 0-8362-2726-3
Library of Congress Catalog Card Number: 96-86641

For David, Joel, and Jason,
whose love and support
have made all things
seem possible

· Contents ·

· Acknowledgments ·

INCALCULABLE THANKS go to my husband, David, for his wonderful sense of adventure and unending faith that have spurred me way beyond my initial horizons. Thanks to my dear friend Sharon Kramis for expanding my culinary experience and for her ongoing support and good counsel. To Betty "Sparky" Boxall, who taught me so much and inspired me to follow my love for cooking and teaching. My sincere thanks to Joyce and Richard Carnovale for sharing their knowledge and passion for the foods, as well as the back roads, of Italy. To Faith Willinger, who has shared with so many her encyclopedic knowledge and love for Italian food and culture. To my friend Marita Adair, who opened a new door for me and whose guidance was invaluable throughout this project. And to Barbara Rodriguez for her kind encouragement, sensitive editing, and infinite patience.

· Foreword ·

You've ARRIVED at last in Italy, but jet lag is definitely taking its toll. What you could use is a nice, comforting meal—nothing too formal, a little soup or pasta, perhaps a glass of wine. That little place on the corner looks pretty good—it says BAR-CAFFÈ (bar kah FEH), and it looks like a bar, but can you eat there, too? If only your friend Giovanni could have come on the trip with you—he speaks Italian and knows all about Italian food. Well, Giovanni couldn't make it, but you've brought along another friend, *The Hungry Traveler: Italy*. It's part of a series of small-format, carry-along guides, and it's packed full with information on menus, restaurants, and easily referenced food terms.

The Hungry Traveler guides are designed to help you find and cross-reference key words in English and the language in which you are ordering your meal. In our *Hungry Traveler: Italy*, you look up the word "Soup" in the Comfort Foods chapter and you find a cross-reference to *Minestra* (mee NES trah) along with a listing of several classic soups and the phonetic pronunciation for each Italian word or phrase. Check out *Minestra* in the Menu Primer chapter and you find many listings and a cross-reference to the "Soup" entry. In addition to key ingredients, you'll find entries for appetizers, entrées, herbs and spices, classic preparations, and beverages.

Missing the tastes of home? In the mood for something a little less exotic? Many of Italy's dishes are very familiar because they've been adopted by America—pizza, spaghetti, and macaroni are among the most obvious examples. In our Comfort Foods chapter, we tell you how the *panino* (pah NEE noh), or sandwich, might differ from those offered back home at the corner deli.

With *The Hungry Traveler* guide in your pocket, you'll have help searching out the "don't-miss" foods of the area. The Regional/Seasonal chapter addresses local, regional, and seasonal specialties with fascinating background information on such subjects as balsamic vinegar, truffles, and the world's best Parmesan cheese—*parmigiano-reggiano* (pahr mee JAHN oh reh JAHN oh). And then there's the wine! Of course you'll want to sample the wines of the different regions, so in the Beverage guide we've provided an overview of the native wines that taste best with the foods of the region. Other beverages are covered as well, including *grappa* (GRAH pah), that high-test alcohol distillate that is often bottled in beautiful clear-glass containers.

Don't miss Market Buying Tips, the chapter on shopping the specialty food shops and markets. It includes tips on purchasing items to take along on your picnic or to stock your touring car or hotel room. And remember to bring an extra bag for those specialty items you'll want to take back home.

The joy of discovery awaits! The myriad contrasts that exist under the deceivingly simple heading of "Italian food" afford you, the Hungry Traveler, a wealth of new experiences. To immerse yourself in the *cucina*—the cooking—is to develop a deeper understanding of the culture and history of this fascinating country and to bask in the warmth and hospitality of its people. So whether your budget is modest or grand, your time plentiful or limited, these pages will help you make the most of your resources—and hungry for more. *Buon Appetito!*

INTRODUCTION

· ■ ·

Passion—it's the first word that comes to mind when discussing the subject of Italians and their love affair with food. Chauvinism might come to mind as well, for each Italian's first love is the food of his mother, branching out only slightly to the *cucina regionale* (koo CHEE nah ray joh NAH lay), the food of the region. And each region boasts differing customs, traditions, and eating habits that have been influenced by historical forces and conquests as well as by geography, soil, and climate. These, in turn, determine the native ingredients and dishes. This localism is most pronounced in the small towns and villages, but even in the larger cities, where modern influences have wrought many changes, gastronomic traditionalists remain.

One outstanding feature of most restaurants in Italy is their use of seasonal ingredients from the surrounding region (unless the restaurant is one that caters only to tourists in the obvious tourist centers). Check out the colorful markets in the morning to see the local, seasonal produce. You'll know what to order when dinnertime comes!

It's helpful to be aware of differing customs and mores and how they might impact your day. When to eat, and where, are some of your first decisions. Your hotel will usually offer a leisurely continental breakfast consisting of your choice of *caffè* (kah FEH), espresso, *cappuccino* (kah poo CHEE noh), or *caffè latte* (kah FEH LAT tay), American-style coffee with a pitcher of milk, along with an assortment of fresh rolls and croissants. For Italians in the cities, breakfast—*colazione*—is often a quick affair, served in the *bar-caffè*. Customers stand up at the bar, order a cappuccino (drunk in the morning, *not* after a meal) or a quick *caffè* and a fresh pastry. Choose your pastry, proceed to the cashier, state your order, pay, and present your receipt to the barman, to whom you'll repeat your order. Try it—it's worth the trouble—you'll be rewarded with a great opportunity to soak up a little of the local culture.

Lunch—*colazione* (kohl ah tzee OH nay)—can be serious business. For most Italians, this is the biggest meal of the day. Lunchtime begins around 12:30 or 1:00 P.M. Just about all commerce shuts down for what may seem like an interminable two to three hours, so plan your shopping accordingly.

But don't fret—if your wallet or schedule dictates otherwise, there are many more modest options. Sandwich bars—*paninoteca* (pah nee noh TEH kah)—provide a quick, inexpensive lunch with either ready-made or made-to-order sandwiches available. Bakeries and pizzerias sell pizza by the slice and savory flat breads—*focaccia* (foh KAHCH chyah) or *schiacciata* (skyaht CHYAH tah), often topped with roasted vegetables and fresh herbs. You can buy picnic fare at grocery stores and specialty food shops dubbed *gastronomia* (gas tron oh MEE ah), *alimentari* (ah lee men TAH ree), or *salumeria* (sah loo may REE ah), where you'll find fresh-baked breads, tantalizing cold cuts and cheeses of the region, prepared salads, olives, and bottles of wine or mineral water. And you might as well drop by the *pasticceria* (pahs tee chay REE ah), or pastry shop, for a little something sweet! This is an option ideal for days spent traveling through the countryside.

Midafternoon cries out for *gelato* (jay LAH toh), available at the *gelateria* (jay lah teh REE ah). This is the rich, smooth ice cream that comes in a dizzying number of intense flavors.

If lunch was light, you'll be ready to attack the Italian menu at night. Dinner—*cena* (CHAY nah), or *pranzo* (PRAHN tsoh)—is served from 7:30 P.M., but no self-respecting Italian would appear before 8:30. If the mood strikes, do as the Italians do and stop first in the *bar-caffè* for a drink, then go on to dinner.

If you've chosen a casual, inexpensive restaurant, a *trattoria* (traht toh REE ah) or *osteria* (ohs teh REE ah), often there is no written menu. The day's specials may be scribbled on a blackboard, or the waiter may give verbal suggestions. In the *trattorias*, dining is informal; you can often order just appetizers and perhaps a bowl of soup. Bring cash, not credit cards, to these establishments. At a *ristorante* (rees toh RAHN teh)—the term reserved for a full-scale dining experience—there's a tablecloth on the table, a written menu is presented, and you will be expected to order three to four courses. A few tips will help you navigate these new waters.

The meal generally consists of four courses, but a more elaborate dinner can expand to six or even eight! The first course—*Il Primo* (eel PREE moh), or *primo piatto* (PREE moh PYAHT toh)—usually consists of soup, pasta (either with a sauce or in a soup), or a rice dish. (Remember to pace yourself!)

The main (second) course—*Il Secondo* (eel sey KON doh)—highlights meat or fish. Portions tend to be rather small. Animal proteins were traditionally festive treats, not the main event on the daily dinner table. Besides, you probably aren't ravenous at this point. Chicken, beef, lamb, veal, and wild game, as well as fish from the local waters or even a substantial vegetable dish, can appear here. Italian law requires that menus divulge if any food, such as fish, has been frozen. The term *surgelato*, meaning "frozen," will tip you off to this fact.

The next course is the side dish of vegetables—*I Contorno* (kon TOR noh) (literally, "contours"—as they round out the meal)—which can consist of substantial dishes of potatoes, mushrooms, eggplant, green beans, fennel, or a light green salad dressed very simply at the table with olive oil (naturally) and a wine vinegar.

And finally the sweet course—*I Dolci* (ee DOHL

chee)—often a bowl of fresh fruit—*frutta fresca* (FROOT tah FRES kah)—or one of the many Italian desserts based on local products such as hazelnuts, almonds, chestnuts, or ricotta, which is similar to cottage cheese. These sweets are often saved for special occasions. Cheese—*formaggio* (for MAHD joh)—is another alternative to end the meal. A cheese course—*Formaggi* (for MAHD jee)—is sometimes offered before the dessert. *Parmigiano* and pecorino (sheep's cheese, which can be either fresh or aged) are generally offered, along with locally made specialties. Assorted cheeses—*formaggi assortiti* (ah sore TEE tee)—may be offered to you on a platter from which you can make a selection. Along with the *parmigiano* and pecorino, a good selection will include gorgonzola (the creamy blue cheese of Italy), *groviera Svizzero* (Swiss cheese), and perhaps the smooth, mild Italian fontina.

In addition, one of the great joys of the Italian table is to begin the meal with the optional appetizer course—*Antipasto* (ahn tee PAS toh)—which can be as simple as a few pieces of the regional *salumi* (sah LOO mee) (a general term referring to all cured meats), a bowl of olives, or perhaps a more elaborate display with mouth-watering marinated vegetables, stuffed zucchini, or eggplant. The cost of the antipasto usually depends on your selections, as well as quantities, and is marked "p.v." (price to be seen) or "s.q." (as to the quantity). Soups can be listed separately under *Minestre* (mee NES treh) or as part of the *primo piatto* (PREE moh PYAHT toh).

One of the best features of the Italian menu is its versatility. In some cases, the waiter will ask you for your order and expect you to decide just on your first course. Decisions for your next courses can be made as the meal progresses, allowing you to customize your meal. You may wish to begin with antipasto and, if it is particularly robust, then decide to skip the pasta course in anticipation of that intriguing lamb stew. Vegetarians will find lots to choose from on the Italian menu, even in the second course. Hearty vegetable dishes such as frittatas (Italian omelettes) or huge porcini, one of the many types of wild Italian mushrooms, oven-roasted, come under this heading.

By the way, almost all restaurants include a cover charge in the total price; it's listed on the menu as *coperto* (koh PAIR toh), and it covers the place setting, clean tablecloth, and bread. In addition, a service charge—*servizio* (seyr VEE tsee oh)—of usually 10 to 12 percent is added to the total cost of your dinner. A small tip in cash, a *mancia* (MAN chah), is normally left on the table if the service has pleased you. If the service charge is as much as 15 percent, one small note (about lire 3,000 or about $2.00 U.S.) is sufficient. Credit cards are becoming more common, especially in the large cities, but be aware that many restaurants do not accept them and plan accordingly.

MENU PRIMER A TO Z
(ITALIAN TO ENGLISH)

· ■ ·

Abbacchio (ahb BAH kyoh). Very young milk-fed lamb (about one month old), traditionally served in Italy for Easter to celebrate and welcome in the spring. This incredibly tender lamb is roasted and usually flavored with garlic and rosemary or sage. *Braciolette d'abbacchio* (brah cho LET teh) are grilled lamb chops, and *costolette d'abbacchio, alla griglia* (kos toh LET teh . . . ah lah GREEL yah) denotes grilled or broiled lamb cutlets or chops. When roasted, they might be designated *al forno* (FOR noh). One of the most popular dishes made from lamb is called *abbacchio allo scottadito* (scot tah DEE toh), which literally means "to scald the fingers." Tiny (hot!) grilled lamb chops are picked up with the fingers, and they make a wonderful appetizer. When lamb is spit-roasted, the menu will say *allo spiedo* (SPYEY doh). (See *Agnello* below and Regional/ Seasonal Specialties: Abruzzo: *Agnello alla griglia* and *Agnello all'uovo e limone,* Lazio: *Agnello,* and Sardegna: *Agnello al finocchio.*)

Acciughe (ah CHOO geh). Anchovy, an indispensable ingredient in several well-known dishes, especially in the southern regions. They're an integral part of *bagna cauda* (BAHN yah KOW dah), that assertive dip for raw vegetables from the Piemonte (Piedmont) region, as well as the infamous *spaghetti alla puttanesca* (poot tan ES kah), or harlot's-style spaghetti. (See *Bagna cauda* and *Pasta/Salse* below and Regional/Seasonal Specialties: Liguria: *Acciughe marinate*.)

Aceto (ah CHAY toh). Vinegar.

Aceto balsamico (ah CHAY toh bahl SAHM ee koh). Balsamic vinegar, the darling of trendy restaurants here in America but in Italy a centuries-old artisan-made vinegar produced solely in Emilia-Romagna's provinces of Modena and Reggio. No other areas have succeeded in reproducing the true *balsamico*. It's made from boiled-down grape must, then aged in a succession of wooden barrels, each made from a different wood. (See Regional/Seasonal Specialties: Emilia-Romagna, Introduction and Market Buying Tips: *Aceto balsamico*.)

Acquacotta (AH kwah KOHT tah). Literally, "cooked water." A vegetable soup from Toscana. (See Regional/Seasonal Specialties: Toscana: *Acquacotta*.)

Affettato misto (ah feh TAH toh MEES toh). This is a popular antipasto of mixed, sliced *salumi* (sah LOO mee), or cold cuts.

Affumicato (ah foo mee KAH toh). Smoked.

Aglio (AL yoh). Garlic.

Agnello (ah NYEL loh). Lamb, the term referring to the slightly older animal as opposed to the one-month-old *abbacchio*. One of the most frequently encountered dishes is *agnello arrosto* (ah ROHS toh), also referred to as *al forno*. This is roast lamb, and it usually refers to leg of lamb. This simple way of preparing lamb, usually flavored with a little olive oil, garlic, and herbs such as rosemary, is often spectacular. *Cotoletta alla milanese* (kot oh LET teh ah lah mee lah NAY zay) is a breaded and fried chop, Milan style. (See *Cotoletta alla Milanese*.) *Alla griglia* indicates the meat was cooked on the grill. Another common dish is *spiedini* (spyey DEE nee). This is shish kebab, which consists of cubes of lamb cooked on a skewer, possibly with skewered vegetables or bacon. (See Regional/ Seasonal Specialties: Lazio: *Agnello* and Sardegna: *Agnello al finnocchio*.)

Agnolotti (ahn yoh LOH tee). A type of pasta. (See *Pasta* below.)

Agrodolce (ahg roh DOL chay). Sweet and sour. The term refers to dishes cooked with sugar and vinegar. The vegetable dish of Sicilia, caponata, is an example, but this preparation can be used for meats and fish as well. (See *Caponata* below.)

Aio e oio (AH yoh ay OH yoh). Garlic and oil sauce. A classic that can employ garlic either in its raw state or quickly cooked. It's served with thin spaghetti and usually includes hot red chili pepper as well. The dish is a staple in Rome.

Al dente (DEN tay). Literally translated as "to the tooth," it's the proper way to cook pasta so it's still slightly chewy and gives slight resistance to the tooth.

Al forno (FOR noh). Roasted. *Forno* is an oven.

Albicocca (ahl bee KOH kah). Apricot.

Alici (ah LEE chee). Anchovies, which in Italy can be found either fresh or salt-cured. This term generally applies to the fresh ones, while *acciughe* could indicate either the fresh or the salt-cured.

Alloro (ahl LOH roh). Laurel, or bay leaf.

Amaretti (ah mah REHT tee). Italian macaroon cookies made with both sweet and bitter almonds, found extensively in the regions of Piemonte and Lombardia.

Ananas (ah nah NAHS). Pineapple.

Anatra (AH nah tra). Duck. *Farcita* (far CHEE tah) indicates that a dish is stuffed, often with sausage and rice. *Petto* (PEYT toh) refers to the breast of duck. (See Regional/Seasonal Specialties: Veneto: *Anatra col pien*.)

Anguilla (ahn GWEEL lah). This is eel, and you might see them *live* in the markets. The newborn "elvers," or *cee* (CHAY), are available only in the spring. When the menu says *in umido* (OO mee doh), they're braised, usually with onion, parsley, and tomato paste. (See Regional/Seasonal Specialties: Lazio: *Anguille,* Toscana: *Anguilla alla fiorentina,* Umbria: *Anguilla alla brace,* and Veneto: *Anguilla alla spiedo*.)

Animelle (ah nee MEHL leh). Sweetbreads.

Antipasto (ahn tee PAS toh) (plural *antipasti*). This is the appetizer course, which comes "before the pasta." The Italian repertoire can range from simple to extremely elaborate. Antipasti are often vegetarian-based; olives, salads, *bruschetta* (broos KET tah), stuffed vegetables such as zucchini and eggplant, *crostini* (kros TEE nee) with an assortment of toppings, and flatbreads are typical. Cured meats (*salumi*) are very common antipasti, including prosciutto (pro SHOOT toh) wrapped around melon or breadsticks called *grissini* (gree SEE nee). In coastal regions, seafood is usually featured. The selection can be astounding—the trick is to pace yourself! (See Introduction and *Bruschetta, Caciu, Caponata, Crostini, Olive ripiene,* and *Salumi* below.)

Antipasti assortiti (ahn tee PAS tee ah sor TEE tee). Assorted appetizers.

Antipasti misti (ahn tee PAS tee MEE stee). Mixed appetizers.

Aperitivo (ah peh ree TEE voh). The aperitif is a drink that precedes dinner, and it is designed to stimulate the appetite. Examples include *Campari* (kahm PAR ee) and the well-known *Cinzano* (chin TSAN oh), the famous brand of vermouth. Many are flavored with bark, herbs, and roots, and they are said to be habit-forming. (See Beverages A to Z: *Aperitivi*.)

Aragosta (ah rah GOHS tah). This is the spiny clawless lobster, found in abundance along the jagged coast of Sardegna. They're a specialty of the coastal town of Alghero, where they are usually served in a salad, simply dressed with lemon and olive oil or with the addition of tomato and onion. They are also cooked with greens such as the ubiquitous wild fennel.

Arancia (ah RAN chah). Orange (the fruit). (See Comfort Foods: Fruit.)

Arista (ah REES tah). Roast loin of pork. This delicious roast was traditionally a treat served only in January, when the pigs were slaughtered. The loin and ribs were cooked fresh, seasoned according to the region (perhaps with juniper berries and bay leaf or rosemary and garlic), while the rest of the pig was preserved in one form or other such as salami and *prosciutto* (pro SHOOT toh) to see the family through the year. (See Comfort Foods: Pork.)

Arrabbiata (all') (ahr rah BYAH tah). A preparation in which hot red chili peppers are cooked with tomatoes and garlic and sometimes other ingredients such as *pancetta* (bacon). *Arrabbiata* means "angry," and it's the fiery red chilies that gave the sauce its name. It can be served with pasta or meats such as *braciole*, thinly sliced steaks. (See Regional/Seasonal Specialties: Lazio: *Pasta: Penne all'arabbiata*.)

Arrosto (ah ROAS toh). Roasted, or the word can also refer to a roast, usually veal, beef, or pork. *Morto al forno* (MOR toh ahl FOR noh) refers to a dish roasted in the oven.

Arsella (ahr SEL lah). A type of wedge-shaped clam from the waters around Sardegna. They may appear with pasta, usually spaghetti, or as part of a mixed fried seafood dish.

Asiago (ah SYAH goh). This is a hard, dry cheese with a pungent flavor made from cow's milk. It's a specialty of the region of Veneto.

Asparagi (ahs PAH rah jee). Asparagus.

Assortiti (ah sor TEE tee). Assorted.

Astice (ahs TEE chay). Lobster, the one with the claws as opposed to the *aragosta*. They are not found in water surrounding Italy but imported—often from the U.S. When they are prepared *armoricaine* (ahr moh ree KAY neh), they're topped with the famous sauce from Armorique, an area of Brittany famous for its lobsters. The sauce is made by cooking onion, carrot, and garlic in olive oil, adding lobster shells (to extract their flavor), brandy, tomatoes, fish stock, and herbs. The sauce is strained, then thickened with flour.

Baccalà (bah kah LAH). Dried, salt-cured cod, which tastes a whole lot better than it sounds! This centuries-old means of preserving fish provided a protein source for the poor. To restore the fish to an edible state, one must first soak it in cold water for one to two days to rehydrate it and remove the salt. The cook can then proceed as with fresh fish. Preparations differ according to region.

- *Bolognese, alla* (boh loh NYAY zay) indicates the fish is cooked in a sauce of lemon, garlic, and parsley.
- *Fritto* (FREET toh) means fried—usually breaded then deep-fried.
- *Genovese, alla* (jen oh VAY zay). As it's cooked in Genoa, with tomato sauce.
- *Livornese, alla* (lee vor NAY zay). The name usually means that it's braised with lemon, garlic,

parsley, white wine, and sometimes slices of cooked tripe.

- *Mantecato* (mahn teh KAH toh). A favorite in Veneto, it's a dish with surprisingly delicate flavor. The cod is boiled in milk and then whipped with olive oil, parsley, and garlic to a creamy consistency, somewhat like firm mashed potatoes. It's served warm as a first course, with a wedge of grilled polenta on which to spread it.
- *Napoletana, all'uso* (nah pohl eh TAHN ah, ahl OO soh). In Naples, it's Neapolitan-style, baked with garlic, parsley, capers, olives, and bread crumbs.
- *Peperoni, con* (pey pey ROH nee). With sweet peppers.
- *Stocco all'anconetana* (STOK koh ahl ahn koh nay TAHN nah). A specialty in Marche, where the cod is braised, this time with tomatoes, olive oil, and white wine. (See *Pesce* below.)
- *Vicentina, alla* (vee chen TEE nah). In the style of Veneto, where the fish is first floured and browned in oil with onions, then braised with milk, onions, anchovies, garlic, and parsley.

Bacelli (bah CHEL lee). The Tuscan word for fava beans.

Bagna cauda (BAH nyah KAW dah). From Piemonte, it's a dip for raw vegetables made with hot olive oil and anchovies. (See *Acciughe* above and Regional/Seasonal Specialties: Piemonte: *Bagna cauda*.)

Barbabietola (bar bah BYEH toh lah). Beet.

Basilico (bah SEE lee koh). Basil. This is the pungent herb that's the basis of pesto, and it just doesn't get any better than in Liguria, birthplace of this now world-renowned sauce. (See *Pesto* below and Regional/Seasonal Specialties: Liguria: Introduction and *Pesto*.)

Bel paese (bel pah AY zay). A mild cow's milk cheese, made in Lombardia.

Bianchetti (byahn KET tee). Tiny anchovy or sardine fry (we're talking small-fry!) are served either fried or boiled and flavored with lemon and olive oil, mostly in the southern regions.

Bianco (bee AHN koh). White, as in white wine. Can also refer to a preparation that has no fats or seasonings, such as rice or pasta.

Bietola (BYEH toh lah). Swiss chard.

Bigoli (bee GO lee). A type of pasta. (See *Pasta* below.)

Biscotti (bees KOT tee). Cookies or biscuits. In Tuscany, the twice-baked almond cookies are referred to as *Biscotti di Prato* or *Cantucci*. They're hard and crisp and are often served after a meal with *vin santo* (VEEN SAHN toh), the usually sweet dessert wine, or coffee—for dunking the cookies.

Bistecca (bees TEK kah). Technically, this term translates as "beefsteak," but the term can refer to almost any meat. The following are some common preparations:

- *Braciola* (bra CHYO la). Translates as "shoulder chop," but it usually refers to stuffed meat rolls, most often made from top or bottom round, pounded thin. They can be filled with prosciutto (pro SHOOT toh), pine nuts, Parmesan, and parsley, or cheese such as fontina, along with some ham. *Braciola* can be rolled into a sausage shape and cooked in a tomato sauce, or the filling can be placed between two slices of beef, held together with a breading of flour, eggs, and bread crumbs, then fried in olive oil.
- *Brasato al barolo* (bra SAHT oh al bar OH loh). Beef braised in barolo, one of the red wines from the Piemonte region.
- *Cacciatore* (kaht chah TOH reh). Means "hunter's-style," which usually refers to thinly cut pan-fried steaks cooked with tomatoes, mushrooms, and wine or according to the whim of the "hunter" (really the cook).
- *Fiorentina, alla* (fyor en TEE nah). The classic dish from Florence (Firenze), consisting of a grilled

T-bone steak, seasoned with pepper, cooked over wood or charcoal, then flavored with garlic, sea salt, and Tuscan olive oil. (See Regional/Seasonal Specialties: Toscana: Introduction and *Bistecca alla fiorentina*.)

- *Pizzaiola, alla* (peet tzah YOH lah). Indicates your steak has been grilled and topped with tomato sauce redolent of oregano, garlic, and parsley.
- *Stracotto* (strah KOT toh). Pot roast, the ultimate comfort food! (See Comfort Foods: Beef.)

Bocconcini (bok kohn CHEE nee). Literally, a "mouthful," this term is used for bite-size chunks of beef, chicken, or veal cooked with white wine, onion, herbs, and sometimes mushrooms and peas.

Bollito (bol LEE toh). Boiled. The term often refers to meats. In the case of boiled chicken, it's *di gallina* (gah LEE nah). *Di manzo* (MAHN zoh) refers to boiled beef.

Bollito misto (bol LEE toh MEES toh). The term refers to a mixture of boiled items. It's a hearty, cold-weather feast usually comprised of an array of boiled meats from the region, such as chicken, veal, sausage, pork, or tongue, served with a variety of sauces, including *salsa verde* (SAL sah VAYR day), a green sauce made with capers. (See Regional/Seasonal Specialties: Emilia-Romagna, Lombardia, and Piemonte: *Bollito misto*.)

Bolognese (boh loh NYAY zay). In the style of Bologna. This usually denotes the slow-cooked meaty sauce called *ragù* (rah GOO) that traditionally tops the egg-rich handmade pasta tagliatelle. It's one of the quintessential dishes of Emilia-Romagna. (See *Pasta/Salse-alla bolognese* and *al ragù* below, and Regional/Seasonal Specialties: Emilia-Romagna: *Ragù, Ragù bolognese*.)

Boragine (bor ah JEE neh). Borage, an herb grown in Liguria that has a mild cucumber flavor. It's often used to flavor pasta dough.

Bottarga (bot TAR gah). This is the roe, or eggs, of the mullet, dried and pressed. Its spicy, briny flavor enhances salads and bean dishes. It can also be made from tuna roe. It's used extensively in Sardegna.

Brace (BRAH chay). Embers. The term describes foods that have been grilled over charcoal.

Braciole (bra CHYO lay). The term can refer to a shoulder chop of lamb or pork, but often it's a thin slice of beef from the top or bottom round, filled with cheese and ham, breaded with flour, egg, and bread crumbs, then panfried. (See *Abbacchio* and *Bistecca* above and Regional/Seasonal Specialties: Campania: *Braciole*.)

Branzino (bran TSEE noh). Sea bass. When prepared *ai capperi* (kahp PEH ree), the cook will flour fillets of bass and cook them in olive oil. A sauce of capers, lemon juice, and parsley is made to pour over the top.

Bresaola (bray zah OH lah). The trendy and delicious dried, cured beef that's produced in Lombardia. Served, especially in Milano, as part of the antipasto. (See Regional/Seasonal Specialties: Lombardia: *Bresaola*.)

Brodetto (braw DET toh) or *brodetto di pesce* (dee PAY shay). A light fish soup or stew that's ubiquitous along the Adriatic coast. The varieties of fish vary according to region, but most are cooked with onion, garlic, tomatoes, fresh herbs, and white wine. (See *Cacciucco* and *Minestra* below and Regional/Seasonal Specialties: Abruzzo: Introduction, Emilia-Romagna: *Brodetto*, and Le Marche: *Brodetto*.)

Brodo (BRAW doh). Homemade broth or stock made from poultry (often capon) or meat—seldom will you encounter the canned stuff! *Di carne* (dee KAR neh) means meat stock, *di gallina* (dee gahl LEE nah) denotes chicken stock, *di manzo* (dee MAHN zoh) indicates beef broth, and *di pesce* (dee PAY shay) is fish stock. *Di pollo* (dee POL loh) is chicken broth. Delicious homemade stock is the foundation of many of the first-rate dishes of Emilia-Romagna such as *tortellini in brodo*, in which delicious handmade meat-stuffed pasta is served in the broth, or, alternatively, noodles such as *tagliolini* can grace the broth, the unsurpassed Italian kin to chicken noodle soup.

Bruschetta (broos KET tah). Garlic bread in the original Italian style. Coarse bread is toasted, then rubbed with garlic and drizzled with olive oil. (See *Antipasto* above and *Fettunta* below and Regional/Seasonal Specialties: Lazio: *Bruschetta* and Umbria: *Bruschetta*.)

Bucatini (boo kah TEE nee). A type of pasta. (See *Pasta* below.)

Budino (boo DEE noh). Pudding.

Burrida (boor REE dah). The name for the fish stew from the Ligurian coast. (See *Minestra* below and Regional/Seasonal Specialties: Liguria: *Burrida*.)

Burro (BOOR ̣roh). Butter. The term *al burro* refers to foods that are cooked in butter.

Busecca (boo SEK kah). Tripe soup. (See Regional/Seasonal Specialties: Lombardia: *Busecca*.)

Cacciagione (kah chah JOH neh). Wild game. Hunters bring home a wide variety of wild game, generally in the cooler winter months. Especially popular are the hairy, black-bristled wild boar called *cinghiale* (cheen GYAH ley), hare, known as *lepre*

(LAY pray), and birds such as pheasant, *fagiano* (fah GYAH noh).

Cacciatora (kaht chah TOH rah). Chicken, rabbit, or other meats are frequently prepared *alla cacciatora,* literally in the "style of the hunter." It usually means a braised dish cooked with olive oil, wine, tomatoes, mushrooms, and herbs.

Cacciucco (kaht CHOO koh). Here's one more term for fish soup or stew in addition to *brodetto, burrida,* and *zuppa di pesce.* This is the Livornese take on the theme (Livorno, or Leghorn, is a coastal town in Tuscany). The sauce will be made of onion, garlic, tomatoes, and herbs cooked with olive oil and white wine. The fish will vary. Crustaceans and mollusks are essential, but the dish may include red mullet, snapper, rock cod, or sea bass, too.

Cachi (KAH kee). Persimmon.

Cacio (KAH choh). This is a general term for cheese in southern Italy.

Cacio e pepe (KAH choh ay PAY pay). Cheese and pepper, a simple, yet delicious pasta topping found mostly in southern regions.

Caciocavallo (kah chyoh kah VAHL loh). This is usually a cow's milk cheese, although it can be made from sheep's or goat's milk. The cheese is made in the shape of a pear and is found throughout southern Italy. Its taste can range from mild to sharp.

Caciotta (kah CHOHT tah). This soft cheese is made in southern Italy. It's the cheese of Le Marche that Michelangelo doted on, made from a combination of cow's milk and sheep's milk.

Caciu, or *caciocavallo, fritto* (kah CHOO or kah chyoh kah VAHL loh FREET toh). Fried cheese, often flavored with herbs, is served as an antipasto. *Caciocavallo* is a hard, white cheese. Fried or grilled cheeses, including mozzarella and pecorino, are common throughout southern Italy.

Calamari (kah lah MAH reh). Squid. Most commonly served deep-fried as *calamari fritti* (FREET tee) but also found stuffed, *ripieni* (ree PYAY nee), with garlic, anchovies, parsley, and bread crumbs, or *e piselli alla livornese* (ay pee SEL lee ah lah lee vor NAY zay), slow-simmered with tomatoes and peas, Tuscan style.

Caldo (KAHL doh). Literally, hot, but it often indicates that the dish is served warm.

Calzone (kahl TSOH nay). Pizza dough that's filled, then folded over into a half-moon. (See Comfort Foods: Pizza: *Calzone,* and Regional/Seasonal Specialties: Puglia: *Calzone.*)

Cannellini (kahn nel LEE nee). These are white kidney beans found throughout the central regions of Abruzzi, Lazio, Toscana, and Umbria.

Cannelloni (kahn nel LON nee). A type of pasta. (See *Pasta* below.)

Cannoli (kahn NOLE lee). One of the most famous Italian desserts, from Sicilia. They're composed of a crunchy fried pastry shell in a cylindrical shape, filled with a soft, creamy ricotta and sweetened with sugar, candied fruit, and chocolate. (See Regional/Seasonal Specialties: Sicilia: Introduction and *Cannoli*.)

Cantucci (kahn TOO chee). These are dry, crunchy almond cookies of Toscana, served often with *vin santo*, the usually sweet dessert wine.

Cape sante (KAH pay SAHN tay). Scallops, which are often cooked in their shells along with their delicious orange roe.

Capelli d'angelo (kahp PEH lee D'AHN jay loh). A type of pasta. (See *Pasta* below.)

Capocollo (kah poh KOHL loh). One of the most common of the cured pork *salumi* on the antipasto menu, especially in the southern regions of Calabria and Puglia. Umbria makes a fine rendition as well. (See Regional/Seasonal Specialties: Umbria: *Capocollo*.)

Caponata (kah poh NAH tah). A Sicilian sweet and sour eggplant dish served as an appetizer, an accompaniment to a meat, or a sauce for pasta. It's at its best in Palermo in Sicilia. (See Regional/Seasonal Specialties: Sicilia: *Caponata*.)

Cappellini (kahp pel LEE nee). A type of pasta. (See *Pasta* below.)

Capperi (kap PAY ree). Capers, which are actually the buds of the caper flower, grown and used extensively in dishes in southern Italy. The finest capers are said to be from Salina in the Lipari Islands, just off the coast of Sicilia.

Cappon magro (kahp PON MAH groh). Literally, "lean capon." Not a real capon but actually a fish dish in Liguria. (See Regional/Seasonal Specialties: Liguria: *Cappon magro*.)

Cappone (kahp POH neh). Capon is the large, castrated rooster that's very popular in Italy, both for roasting and for making excellent broth.

Capra (KAHP rah). Goat. Baby goat, or kid, *capretto* (kah PRET toh), is traditionally served in the spring. *Capriolo* (kahp ree OH loh) is the word for "roebuck." (See Regional/Seasonal Specialties: Emilia-Romagna: *Capretto* and Trentino–Alto Adige: *Capriolo*.)

Caprino (kap PREE noh). Goat cheese.

Carabaccia (kah rah BAH chyah). This is the name for onion soup in Toscana.

Carbonara (kar boh NAH rah). Literally, "coalman's style." Named for the woodsmen who were charcoal makers; they would take this hearty dish along for their lunch. The rich sauce is made with bacon and eggs and is most often served with spaghetti. (See *Pasta/Salse* below and Regional/Seasonal Specialties: Lazio: *Pasta: spaghetti alla carbonara*.)

Carciofi (kahr CHOH fee). Artichokes are an especially popular vegetable in Italy, where they are eaten primarily in the spring when they are young and tender. They can be eaten raw, trimmed and thinly sliced, in a salad. (See Regional/Seasonal Specialties: Lazio: *Carciofi alla Giudia, Carciofi alla romana*.)

Cardi (KAR dee). The cardoon is a popular vegetable in the regions of Abruzzo, Molise, and Piemonte. Although actually a member of the artichoke family, the cardoon resembles thick stalks of celery. The flavor is more like that of an artichoke, however. In Piedmont, it's used raw, trimmed and dipped in the Piedmontese dip called *bagna cauda*. In other regions, it's served cooked, usually fried.

Carne (KAHR nay). This is the generic word for meat, but it usually refers to beef.

Carpa or *carpione*. (KAHR pah, or kahr PYO neh). Carp, a fish found in the fresh waters of Lago di Trasimeno in Umbria. (See Regional/Seasonal Specialties: Umbria: *Regina in porchetta*.)

Carpaccio (kahr PAH chyoh). Raw beef, very thinly sliced, and served with shaved *parmigiano* and an olive oil dressing. Named for the Venetian Renaissance painter Vittore Carpaccio, who was known for his use of vivid reds and whites. Note: Although reports of illness resulting from raw meats have not surfaced, diners should always be aware of the risk when eating such dishes. (See Regional/Seasonal Specialties: Piemonte: *Insalata di carne cruda*.)

Carta da musica (KAHR tah dah MOO zee kah). A thin, crisp crackerlike bread from Sardegna. (See Regional/Seasonal Specialties: Sardegna: *Carta da musica*.)

Casa, della (KAH sah). Literally, "of the house," it means a specialty of the restaurant, made with the ingredients available and according to the whims of the cook.

Casalinga, alla (kah sah LEEN gah). Literally, "in the style of the housewife," but it suggests home-style food.

Cassata (kah SAH tah). A dessert specialty of Sicilia made with sweetened ricotta, sponge cake, almond paste, candied fruit, and liqueur. (See Regional/Seasonal Specialties: Abruzzo: *Cassata abruzzese* and Sicilia: *Cassata siciliana*.)

Castagna (kas TAHN yah). Chestnut, which is often made into chestnut flour for unusual desserts like *monte bianco* (which translates as "white mountain"), as well as *gelato*.

Cavallo (kah VAHL loh). Horse. Yes, it could be on the menu, especially in Veneto, usually braised, like beef, with vegetables, broth, and wine!

Caviale (kah VYAH leh). Caviar.

Cavolfiore (kah vol FYO reh). Cauliflower.

Cavolo (kah VOH loh). Cabbage.

Ceci (CHEH chee). Chickpeas.

Cee, or *Cieche alla pisana* (CHEY, or CHAY kay ah lah pee SAH nah). Baby eels, cooked in a sauce of tomatoes and garlic and topped with Parmesan, a very popular dish in Toscana.

Cervello (cher VEHL loh). Brains.

Cervo (CHER voh). Venison.

Cetrioli (che tree OH lee). Cucumbers.

Cetrioli sott'aceto (che tree OH lee soht tah CHAY toh). Pickles.

Chiacchiere (kee ahk KYAY reh). From the verb "to chat," these delicious strips of dough are deep-fried and sprinkled with confectioners' sugar. They are found in cafés and bars in southern Italy and are served with coffee and, of course, conversation.

Chiocciole (kyoh CHYOH leh). Snails.

Ciabatta (chyah BAHT tah). Bread made in the shape of a slipper.

Ciambella (chyam BEHL lah). Literally, "ring cake." Dozens of versions exist, but generally it's a ring of sweet pastry. (See Regional/Seasonal Specialties: Emilia-Romagna: *Ciambella*.)

Cicoria (chee koh REE ah). Chicory, a curly-leafed, somewhat bitter salad green used widely in salads and pastas, especially in the south.

Cinghiale (cheen GYAH ley). Wild boar, which is highly prized for its rich flavor, especially in Toscana and Umbria. Boar is often braised or rubbed with fresh herbs such as rosemary and fennel and spit-roasted.

Cioccolato (chee ohk koh LAH toh). Chocolate. (See Market Buying Tips: *Cioccolato*.)

Cipolla (chee POL lah). Onion.

Coda alla vaccinara (KO dah ah lah vah chee NAH rah). Oxtail stew, a specialty in Lazio. (See Regional/Seasonal Specialties: Lazio: *Coda alla vaccinara*.)

Conchiglie (kon KEE lyay). A type of pasta. (See *Pasta* below.)

Coniglio (koh NEE lyoh). Rabbit. Usually domestic, but also hunted in the wild. Often served *alla cacciatora* (kaht chah TOH rah), "hunter's-style," a preparation that varies according to region and chef. Generally, it's a stew, braised with tomatoes, onions, sometimes mushrooms, and white wine. (See Regional/Seasonal Specialties: Liguria: *Coniglio* and Le Marche: *Coniglio*.)

Cono (KOH noh). Cone, as for ice cream.

Consommé (KOHN soh meh). This is the familiar clear, strained meat broth (usually beef), which can be adorned with strips of vegetables—*julienne* (joo lee EHN neh) or pasta—*con pastina* (kon pahs TEE nah); or it may be reduced to make it richer—*doppio*, "double" (DOH pyoh), or *ristretto*, "reduced" (rees TREHT toh).

Contorno (kon TOR noh). Vegetable side dishes. Served either with but usually after the *secondo piatto*, or second course. Contorni may consist of a simple salad or (often over-) cooked vegetables such as green beans or greens but can also consist of exquisite dishes like roasted porcini. (See *Porcini* below.)

Coppa (KOP pah). Literally, "cup," and on a menu it can refer to a cup of fruit or to a delicious, boneless, salt-cured ham from Emilia-Romagna. (See Regional/ Seasonal Specialties: Emilia-Romagna: *Coppa*.)

Coppa di frutta (KOP pah dee FROOT tah). Cup of fresh fruit or fruit cocktail.

Costata di bistecca alla fiorentina (kohs TAH tah dee bees TEH kah AH lah fyoh ren TEE nah). Cutlet. (See *Bistecca* above, *Cotoletta* below.)

Cotechino (kot eh KEE noh). Pork sausage (cooked). One of the many *salumi* produced in Lombardia and Emilia-Romagna. (See Regional/Seasonal Specialties: Emilia-Romagna: *Cotechino*.)

Cotto (KOT toh). Cooked.

Cotoletta (kot oh LET tah), or *costoletta* (kos toh LET tah). Cutlet. (See Regional/Seasonal Specialties: Lombardia: *Cotoletta alla milanese* and Valle d'Aosta: *Cotoletta alla Valdostana*.)

Cozze (KOH tsay), or *muscoli* (MOO skoh lee). These are the mussels with the bluish-black shell and orange flesh. They're often served *all'agro* (AH groh), which is simply with lemon juice. When listed as *arrosto* (ah ROAS toh), the mussels are usually steamed first, then baked or grilled on the half shell with bread crumbs, herbs, and sometimes ham, cheese, and tomato sauce.

Crema (KREH mah). Does not refer to the cream for your *caffè*, that's *panna* (PAHN nah). *Crema* can denote a custard, a creamed soup, or a flavor of ice cream. *Crema gianduja* (jahn DOO yah) is a creamy spread of chocolate and hazelnuts that may replace peanut butter in your heart forever! The mixture can also be the filling for chocolates, called *giandujotti* (jahn doo YOT tee), a specialty of Turino. (See Regional/Seasonal Specialties: Piemonte: Introduction and *Gianduja* and Market Buying Tips: *Cioccolato*.)

Crespelle (kres PEL leh). Crepes.

Crostata (kros TAH tah). Fruit tart, usually open-faced, sometimes with a lattice top, and filled with the fresh fruit of the season.

Crostini (krohs TEE nee). Thin rounds of toast, served as an antipasto. (See Regional/Seasonal Specialties: Toscana: *Crostini al fegato* and Umbria: *Crostini*).

Crudo (KROO doh). Raw.

Cucina (koo CHEE nah). This technically means the "kitchen," but it also denotes the particular cuisine of a region, as in *pollo alla romana.*

Datteri di mare (DAT tay ree dee MAH ray). "Sea dates." A type of clam.

Delizie (day LEE tsyay). Literally, "delights." Refers to all sorts of specialty foods.

Diavolo (dee AH voh loh). Deviled. Usually assigned to dishes that are made fiery hot with red peppers. *Diavolicchio* (dee ah voh LEE kyoh) is the incredibly hot condiment of the southern regions, made with the fiery hot peppers called *peperoncini.*

Digestivo (dee jes TEE voh). This is an after-dinner drink, an essential to proper digestion. (See Beverages A to Z: *Digestivi.)*

Dolce (DOL chay). Sweet. *I Dolce* refers to the sweet or dessert course.

Dragoncello (dra gon CHEL loh). Tarragon.

Erba (AIR bah). Herb.

Etto (ET toh). A measure of weight used in restaurants, where you may be charged by the weight of an item (for instance, lobster), and in a store. It equals about three and a half ounces.

Fagiano (fah GYAH noh). Pheasant.

Fagioli (fah JOH lee). Beans, like the white *cannellini* that are a staple of the Tuscan kitchen. Dried beans are used extensively in Italian cooking, as in the popular soup *pasta e fagioli*.

Fagiolini (fah joh LEE nee). String beans.

Faraona (fahr AH OH nah). Guinea fowl.

Farfalle (fahr FAH leh). A type of pasta. (See *Pasta* below.)

Farina (fah REE nah). Flour.

Farro (FAR roh). Emmer, a wheaty-tasting grain used by the ancient Romans and still popular today. Used in making hearty soups, especially in southern Umbria. (See *Minestra di farro* below, Regional/Seasonal Specialties: Umbria: *Minestra di farro*, and Market Buying Tips: *Farro*.)

Fave (FAH vay). Fava beans. The small young beans appear in the springtime and are favored by the Romans in salads or eaten with *pecorino romano* (sheep's milk cheese).

Fegatelli (feg ah TEL lee). Pork liver.

Fegatini (feg ah TEE nee). Chicken livers.

Fegato (feh GAH toh). Calf's liver. When the menu reads *fegato alla veneziana* (veh neets YAH nah), the dish is cooked with onions and served over polenta. The Venetians claim it, but it's available all over Italy. (See Regional/Seasonal Specialties: Toscana: *Crostini al fegato* and Veneto: *Fegato alla veneziana*.)

Ferri, ai ferri (ay FER ree). Literally "on iron," or grilled. This preparation is used for fish as well as meat. The preparation usually involves a marinade of olive oil and herbs, which is used again to baste the fish or meat as it cooks on the grill.

Fettuccine (feh too CHEE nee). A type of pasta. (See *Pasta* below.)

Fettunta (fet TOON tah). The Tuscan name for *bruschetta*, or garlic bread. (See *Bruschetta* above and Regional/Seasonal Specialties: Toscana: *Fettunta*.)

Finocchiella (fee noh KYEL lah). This world-renowned pork sausage of Umbria is flavored with fennel seeds.

Finocchio (fee NOK yoh). Fennel, the licorice-flavored vegetable, is eaten both raw in salads and cooked.

Finocchiona (fee nok YONE nah). This exceptional Tuscan version of pork sausage is flavored with fennel seeds.

Focaccia (foh KAH chyah). This is flatbread, also known as *schiacciata* or *pizza bianca*. It's essentially pizza crust, which is baked plain or with herbs and onion.

Fonduta (fon DOO tah). The northern Italian take on fondue, made with fontina. (See Regional/Seasonal Specialties: Piemonte: *Fonduta con tartufo*, Valle d'Aosta: *Fonduta*, and Market Buying Tips: *Formaggi* and *Fontina*.)

Fontina (fon TEE nah). A fabulous, buttery-flavored cheese produced in the Valle d'Aosta region. Age-old production techniques are still in practice today. Aficionados actually prefer fontina made using milk from cows who have grazed in the mountain pastures on tender spring grasses (as opposed to the more mature grasses of summer and fall). Fontina has great melting properties and so is used in *fonduta*, the Italian version of fondue. (See Regional/Seasonal Specialties: Piemonte: *Fonduta con tartufo*, Valle d'Aosta: *Fonduta*, and Market Buying Tips: *Formaggi* and *Fontina*.)

Formaggio (for MAHD joh). Cheese. Italy produces many fine cheeses, and a cheese course is often included on the menu. Some of the better-known cheeses of Italy are fontina, gorgonzola, mozzarella, *parmigiano-reggiano*, *pecorino romano*, and ricotta, but hundreds of cheeses that Italy produces are never exported and definitely merit sampling! (See *Asiago*, *Bel paese*, *Caciocavallo*, *Caciotta*, and *Fontina* above,

Gorgonzola, Grana, Mascarpone, Mozzarella, Parmigiano-reggiano, Pecorino, Provolone, Ricotta, Scamorza, and *Taleggio* below and Regional/Seasonal Specialties: Basilicata: *Buratta* and *Provola* and Market Buying Tips: *Formaggi.*)

Forno (FOR noh). Oven. *Al forno* refers to something that's been baked or roasted in the oven.

Fragole (FRAH go lay). Strawberries. *Fragoline* (frah goh LEE nay) are the exquisitely flavored small wild strawberries.

Freddo (FRED doh). Cold.

Friarelli (free ah REL lee). Broccoli.

Frittata (freet TAH tah). The pan-cooked omelette of Italy. It includes eggs, assorted vegetables such as artichokes and zucchini (usually according to the season, or the whim of the cook), cheese, and herbs.

Frittella (free TEHL lah). Fritter, or pancake.

Fritto misto (FREET toh MEES toh). Literally, "mixed fry." A mix of fried foods that can vary according to the location or the season. It may include seafood or meats and an assortment of vegetables. (See Regional/Seasonal Specialties: Campania: *Fritto misto di pesce,* Lazio: *Fritto misto alla romana,* Piemonte: *Fritto misto,* and Toscana: *Fritto misto alla fiorentina.*)

Frittura di mare (freet TOO rah DEE MAH ray) or *di pesce* (dee PAY shay). A mixture of fried seafood.

Frutta (FROOT tah). Fruit. *Frutta cotta* (KOT tah) is fruit stewed with wine and spices.

Frutti di bosco (FROOT tee dee BOS koh). The literal translation is "fruits of the forest," but the term generally refers to an assortment of wild berries.

Frutti di mare (FROOT tee dee MAH ray). Literally, "fruits of the sea," but this actually refers to an array of shellfish. (See *Pesce* below.)

Funghi (FOON ghee). Mushrooms. (See *Galletti* and *Porcini* below and Market Buying Tips: *Funghi.)*

Fusilli (foo ZEE lee). A type of pasta. (See *Pasta* below.)

Fuso (FOO soh). Melted.

Galletti (gahl LET tee). Chanterelle (mushrooms).

Gallina (gahl LEE nah). Hen.

Gamberetti (gahm bey RET tee). Small shrimp or prawns. *Gamberi* (gahm BEH ree) are regular-sized prawns, and *gamberoni* (gahm beh ROH nee) refers to the large ones. When boiled, they're tagged *bolliti* (bol LEE tee). They're then served cold, usually with a mayonnaise-based sauce.

Garmugia (gahr MOO jah). A harbinger of spring-time in Toscana, this soup is made with spring vegetables of fava beans, peas, artichokes, asparagus, and *pancetta* (Italian bacon).

Gelato (jay LAH toh). Italian ice cream. Made from whole milk (not cream), sugar, eggs, and flavoring (often fresh fruit at its peak). The number of flavors is staggering. Some of the more unusual include:

- *Bacio* (BAH choh). Chocolate with hazelnut.
- *Castagna* (kah STAHN nyah). Chestnut.
- *Crema* (KREH mah). Egg custard.
- *Gianduja* (jahn DOO yah). Milk chocolate hazelnut cream.
- *Malaga* (mah LAH gah). Rum raisin.
- *Panna* (PAHN nah). Whipped cream.
- *Riso* (REE zoh). Rice pudding.
- *Taroccho* (tah ROH koh). Blood orange.
- *Tiramisù* (tee rah mee SOO). Like the popular dessert trifle.

Fruit flavors abound, and their intensity will amaze the uninitiated. The very best *gelati* are made right at the *gelateria*. You can tell if they're homemade by the presence of stainless steel bins, which are sterilized and reused. Plastic bins are used by commercial producers.

Ghiaccio (GYAHT choh). Ice.

Gianduja (jahn DOO yah). A creamy, delectable mixture of chocolate and hazelnuts. *Giandujotti* (jahn doo YOT tee) are wedges of chocolate with hazelnuts. (See Regional/Seasonal Specialties: Piemonte: Introduction and Market Buying Tips: *Cioccolato*.)

Ginepro (JEEN ay pro). Juniper berry, which is used to flavor hearty wild game sauces.

Gnocchi (NYOH kee). These are dumplings, made most often from cooked mashed potato and flour but often with other ingredients such as stale bread (in which case they're billed *di pane* [dee PAH nay] or sometimes with vegetables such as winter squash. In Toscana, they're commonly made with ricotta and perhaps spinach, and they'll be listed as *di ricotta* (dee ree KOH tah). Sauces vary according to the region, from creamy fontina to piquant pesto. (See Regional/Seasonal Specialties: Friuli–Venezia Giulia: *Gnocchi*, Lazio: *Gnocchi alla romana*, Piemonte: *Gnocchi di patate*, and Valle d'Aosta: *Gnocchi alla valdostara*.)

Gorgonzola (gor gon ZOH lah). The fabulous blue cheese of Italy, produced in the region of Lombardia. The milder, more "approachable" version is called *dolce* (DOL chay). The stronger, classic, more "fragrant" version is termed *piccante* (peek KAN tay). (See Regional/Seasonal Specialties: Lombardia: Introduction and Market Buying Tips: *Formaggi: Gorgonzola*.)

Grana (GRAH nah), or *grana padana* (GRAH nah pah DAH nah). A nutty-flavored, grainy cheese mainly produced in Lombardia. Grana resembles *parmigiano-reggiano* but does not command its respect (or price tag).

Granchio (GRAN kyoh). Crab.

Granita (grah NEE tah). A grainy-textured "Italian ice," usually made either with fresh lemon juice—*limone* (lee MOH neh)—or coffee—*caffè* (kah FAY).

Grano (GRAH noh). Grain.

Granseola (grahn say OH lah). The sea crab of the Adriatic.

Gremolada (grem oh LAH dah). A mixture of fresh parsley, garlic, and lemon peel used to garnish *osso buco* (veal shanks).

Griglia (GREEL yah). Grill. *Alla griglia* indicates the food was cooked on the grill, and it's the same as *ai ferri*.

Grissini (gree SEEN nee). Bread sticks, the very best of which are handmade in Piemonte. (See Regional/Seasonal Specialties: Piemonte: Introduction and Grissini.)

Guanciale (gwan CHAH lay). The meat from the hog's jowl that's used to flavor many dishes, especially soups and pastas.

Insalata (een sah LAH tah). Salad—usually a simple mixed greens salad dressed with olive oil, a little wine vinegar, salt, and pepper. It is most often served after the main course.

Insalata caprese (een sah LAH tah kah PRAY zay). This classic salad originated in Capri, but has gained prominence around the world. It consists of slices of mozzarella (the best is *mozzarella di bufala*—BOO fahl lah), sliced tomato, and fresh basil leaves, drizzled with olive oil. This salad appears on the antipasto menu.

Insalata di mare (een sah LAH tah dee MAH ray), or *Insalata di frutti di mare* (een sah LAH tah dee FROOT tee dee MAH ray). This cold salad of boiled, chilled seafood, dressed with oil and vinegar or lemon juice, is common, especially along the Adriatic coast. (See Regional/Seasonal Specialties: Lazio: *Insalata di mare.*)

Insalata di pesce (een sah LAH tah dee PAY shay). Just other name for fish and/or seafood salad (ingredients can vary widely), dressed either with lemon and olive oil or with a mayonnaise-based sauce.

Insalata mista (een sah LAH tah MEES tah). A mixed greens salad found on the *contorno* part of the menu. It can include whatever vegetables the chef has on hand but usually features tomatoes, radishes, peppers, and onions and is dressed simply with olive oil and perhaps wine vinegar or lemon juice.

Integrale (een teh GRAH leh). Whole wheat.

Involtini (een vohl TEE nee). Boneless fillets of meat, veal, pork, beef, or fowl. Stuffed with a variety of vegetables, then rolled and cooked in a sauce of wine and broth. (See *Vitello* below.)

Lampone (lahm POH neh). Raspberry.

Lardo (LAHR doh). Salt-cured lard that is used as a spread in place of butter in the Piemonte and Valle d'Aosta regions.

Lasagne (lah ZAHN yay). A type of pasta. (See *Pasta* below and Comfort Foods: Pasta.)

Latteria (lah teh REE ah). A broad term that refers to a variety of cow's milk cheeses from Friuli. The younger, softer cheeses are mild, while the more mature ones are firmer and more sharp-tasting. The term can also refer to a shop that sells dairy products.

Lattuga (laht TOO gah). Lettuce.

Lauro (LAHW roh). Laurel, or bay leaf.

Lenticchie (len TEE kyeh). Lentils are one of the most favored legumes in Italy, and they are used in many of the traditional dishes, where they often appear in soups or are served alongside sausage. (See

Minestra di lenticchie below and Market Buying Tips: *Lenticchie*.)

Lepre (LAY pray). Hare, as well as wild rabbit, is quite common on menus throughout the country. (See *Coniglio* above and Regional/Seasonal Specialties: Piemonte: *Lepre in salmi*, Toscana: *Pappardelle*, and Umbria: *Lepre alla olive*.)

Lesso (LES soh). Boiled.

Limone (lee MOH neh). Lemon.

Lingua (LEEN gwah). Tongue.

Linguine (leen GWEE nay). A type of pasta. (See *Pasta* below.)

Livornese, alla (lee vor NAY zay). This refers to a dish that's prepared in the style of the Tuscan town Livorno, usually with lemon, garlic, parsley, and white wine. (See *Baccalà, alla livornese* above.)

Lombatina (lom bah TEE nah). Veal chop.

Lumache (loo MAH keh). Snails. Italy does many takes on the delicacy, depending on the region.

• *Alle nove erbe* (AHL leh NOH vay EHR bay). Indicates that they are cooked with nine herbs. A specialty of Le Marche.

- *Bourguignonne, alla* (boo ghy NOHN nay). The classic way of preparing snails, with garlic butter, in the style of Burgundy, France.
- *Lumache all'origano* (oh ree GHA noh). Snails, Pugliese style, cooked in olive oil with garlic, oregano, mint, salt, and pepper.
- *Romana, alla* (roh MAH nah). Roman style, of course, where they're braised in their shells with a sauce of tomatoes, anchovies, wild mint, garlic, and olive oil.
- *Valdostana, alla* (vahl dos TAH nah). A similar preparation to the Roman recipe, but add mushrooms and herbs and hold the anchovies.

Maccheroni (mah keh ROH nee). A type of pasta. (See *Pasta* below.)

Macedonia (mah chay DOH nyah). Fresh (and sometimes not so fresh!) fruit salad, served for dessert throughout Italy. If possible, check it out before ordering; it's often on display.

Maggiorana (mahd joh RAH nah). Marjoram.

Maiale (mah YAH lay). Pork. One of the more impressive presentations is *arrosto in porchetta* (ah ROAS toh een pore KET tah), in which a whole suckling pig (or a larger pig) is stuffed with various herbs such as rosemary and fennel, as well as garlic, bacon, and the pig's liver. This dish is often spit-roasted. (See Comfort Foods: Pork and Regional/

Seasonal Specialties: Basilicata: *Maiale all'alloro* and *Porchetta* in Lazio and Umbria.)

Malloreddus (mahl loh RED doos). Sardinian gnocchi (NYOH kee), or dumplings. (See Regional/Seasonal Specialties: Sardegna: *Malloreddus.*)

Mandorle (MAHN dor ley). Almonds.

Manzo (MAHN zoh). This term refers to a steer that's been castrated, but just read it as "beef."

- *Battuto di manzo* (baht TOO toh). A hamburger or ground beef.
- *Bistecca di manzo* (bees TAYK kah). Beefsteak.
- *Bollito* (bol LEE toh). Refers to boiled beef, but actually it means "simmered in a fragrant broth until tender."
- *Polpette di manzo* (pol PEHT tay). Meatballs.
- *Stracotto di manzo* (stra KOT toh). Beef pot roast. (See *Brodo* above.)

Marinato (mar ee NAH toh). Marinated.

Marmellata (mahr meyl LAH tah). Marmalade, or jam.

Marroni (mahr ROH nee). Chestnuts are plentiful in the northern regions, and many popular desserts are made with them. Chestnuts were also ground into flour and used by the poor in place of wheat flour. *Marrons glacés* (glah SAY) are the candied chestnuts that were invented in Genoa.

Mascarpone (mahs kahr POH nay). A delicious, rich triple-cream cheese used extensively in desserts such as tiramisù (ter ah mee SOO). (See *Tiramisù* below and Market Buying Tips: *Formaggi: Mascarpone.*)

Mazzancolle (mah tsan KOL leh). Giant prawns.

Medaglione (may dah LYOH nay). This term indicates small rounds of beef or veal steak, cut from the tenderloin, loin, sirloin, or round. When listed as *al barolo* (bah ROH loh), they're braised in a red wine (*barolo*) sauce.

Mela (MEY lah). Apple.

Melanzane (mey lahn TSA nay). Eggplant. (See Comfort Foods: Eggplant Parmesan and Regional/Seasonal Specialties: Calabria: *Melanzane alla scapece* and *Parmigiana di melanzane* and Campania: *Melanzane alla mozzarella* and *Parmigiana di melanzane.*)

Melone (mey LOH nay). This is the general term for melon, but most often it will refer to cantaloupe. It's served as part of the antipasto with a thin slice of prosciutto wrapped around or draped over it.

Menta (MEN tah). Mint.

Merluzzo (mehr LOO tsoh). Fresh rock cod, as opposed to the salted and dried *baccalà*, is often served breaded and fried—*fritto* (FREET toh).

Mezzo (MET tzoh). Half.

Midollo (mee DOHL loh). Bone marrow.

Miele (mee AY lay). Honey.

Milza (MEEL tzah). Spleen. In Toscana, it can appear on *crostini*, or thin toasted bread rounds, as part of the antipasto. It will be minced and sautéed. The taste is similar to the more commonly found chicken liver topping for *crostini*.

Minestra (mee NES trah). Soup. The term can also denote the first course of a meal (usually in the plural form, *minestre*) although soups are generally listed under *primi* (PREE mee), along with pasta and risotto. *Zuppa* (TSOOP pah) is another common name for soup. Soups in Italy run the gamut from elegant, light broth, *brodo* (BRAW doh), made of poultry, beef, or veal (often enhanced with wonderful homemade pasta such as tortellini), to thick, hearty, peasant soups of beans, grains, and vegetables enriched with a little olive oil, a source of warmth and sustenance in the cold of winter. Along the many seacoasts, fish soups abound, each hamlet asserting it makes "the best." They are listed variously as *brodetto* (braw DET toh), *burrida* (boor REE dah), or *zuppa di pesce* (TSOOP pah dee PAY shay), and the ingredient list changes not only from place to place but from day to day, depending on the day's catch. Most soups are economical to make, and for most of the people throughout the ages, they were a way the frugal housewife could stretch meager supplies to feed the family. Yesterday's stale bread was resurrected in dishes such as *pappa col pomodoro* (PAHP pah kol pom oh DAW roh) and *ribollita* (ree bohl LEE tah), and the resulting dishes were so good they remain with us today, in more affluent times. Vegetable soups, of which minestrone (mee nes TROH nay) is probably the best known, are as diverse as the regions from which they come and can be based on either water or broth. Here again, season often plays a role in determining what's on the menu.

- *Minestra di ceci* (mee NES trah dee CHEH chee). Chickpea soup, especially prevalent in the southern regions, usually contains onion, tomato, herbs, and olive oil and can include pasta or rice.
- *Minestra di fagioli* (mee NES trah dee fah JOH lee). Dried bean soup, usually made from *cannellini* or other white beans that are cooked with bacon, onion, garlic, tomatoes, and herbs.
- *Minestra di farro* (mee NES trah dee FAR roh). Hearty soup made with emmer, a wheatytasting grain, and beans. (See *Farro* above, and

Regional/Seasonal Specialties: Umbria: Introduction and *Minestra di farro*.)

- *Minestra di funghi* (mee NES trah dee FOON ghee). Mushroom soup that's generally made with delicious, meaty porcini (por CHEE nee) and combined with onion, garlic, tomatoes, and sometimes barley or chickpeas.

- *Minestra di lenticchie* (mee NES trah dee len TEE kyeh). Lentil soup, in which the lentils are often paired with rice and flavored with the Italian bacon pancetta and tomatoes, then garnished with parsley.

- *Minestra d'orzo* (mee NES trah DOR zoh). Barley soup, which can contain beans, *fagioli*, as well, is a thick, hearty soup prepared by browning onion, bacon, carrot, and celery in olive oil, then adding the barley, tomatoes, and either water or broth. This is a favorite in Trentino–Alto Adige.

- *Minestra pavese* (mee NES trah pah VAY zay). Literally, "poor man's soup," it consists of broth with a slice of grilled toast topped with a poached or fried egg.

- *Minestra alla valdostana* (mee NES trah ah lah vahl dos TAH nah). A regional specialty of Valle d'Aosta, it's made with cabbage and fontina and thickened with stale rye bread.

Minestrone (mee nes TROH nay). A hearty mixed vegetable soup cooked (usually) with beans and either some type of pasta or other starch such as rice or barley. Originating in Lombardia, where the starch is more often rice, the soup has become popular in varying forms all over Italy as well as in American kitchens. In Liguria it's laced with pesto.

Misti (MEES tee). "Mixed," as in *antipasti misti*, mixed appetizers, which usually consist of vegetables, either raw or cooked, or perhaps stuffed, as well as olives and sausage.

Mocetta (moh CHET tah). This is a delicious cured meat, or *salume* (sah LOO may), from the Valle d'Aosta region. In the past, it was made from chamois, but today it's most often made from beef.

Moleche (moh LEH keh). These soft-shelled crabs of Venezia are often served fried.

Monte bianco (MON teh bee AHN koh). A cone-shaped dessert made with pureed fresh chestnuts. (See Regional/Seasonal Specialties: Piemonte: *Monte bianco*.)

Montone (mon TOH nay). Mutton.

Mortadella (mor tah DEHL lah). This is the original "baloney" from Bologna. A finely textured pork sausage with cubes of fat, black peppercorns, and other spices scattered throughout, it's a far superior product to its many imitators. (See Regional/Seasonal Specialties: Emilia-Romagna: *Mortadella*.)

Moscioli (mos CHYOH lee). Mussels. (Also spelled *muscoli*.) (See *Cozze* above.)

Mostarda (mos TAHR dah). It could be mustard, but usually it's a chutneylike mixture made with different fruits that are pickled and mixed with mustard seed. It is served with *bollito misto*.

Mozzarella (motz tzah REHL lah). This familiar fresh, white cheese is found worldwide on pizza and in countless other dishes. The original, made from the rich, creamy milk of buffalo, comes from the region of Campania, of which Naples (birthplace of pizza) is the capital. *Mozzarella di bufala* (BOO fah lah) is still the finest, with a velvety texture and a delicate sweet/savory flavor, but it's a little pricey for everyday use. Today, cow's milk mozzarella, *fior di latte* (FYOR dee LAT tay), is used more widely, but *do* try the buffalo variety if you get a chance. (See *Insalata caprese* above, Regional/Seasonal Specialties: Campania: Introduction, *Melanzane alla mozzarella*, and *Mozzarella in carrozza*, and Market Buying Tips: *Formaggi: Mozzarella*.)

Nepitella (ney pee TEHL lah). This is the herb calamint, a member of the mint family, that grows wild in much of Italy. It is often used to flavor artichokes and mushrooms.

Nocciola (noh CHOH lah). Hazelnut. Wonderful hazelnuts are produced in Italy, especially in Piemonte, where they are found in many special dishes and confections.

Noce (NOH chay). Walnut. The term can also refer to any type of nut.

Nonna, della (NOHN nah). Grandmother's style. The inference is to old-fashioned methods and recipes, but this term can refer to just about any preparation, depending on the grandmother, and, of course, her skill!

Norcina, alla (nor CHEE nah). Norcia is a town in Umbria that specializes in pork products made by artisanal pork butchers. The term generally refers to a dish containing pork (usually wild boar) sausage. (See Regional/Seasonal Specialties: Umbria: *Salsiccia di cinghiale.*)

Olio d'oliva (OL yoh d'oh LEE vah). More than just the fat of choice for cooking and dressing salads, olive oil in Italy is an institution. Even in the north, where butter is abundant, olive oil plays a significant role. Used as a condiment, the fragrant oil can be drizzled over soups and fresh seafood. Crusty bread is rubbed with garlic and anointed with the oil. Spaghetti is often tossed simply with garlic and olive oil. Olive oils are as integral a part of the food of Italy as olive trees are of the landscape. The trees grow throughout most of the peninsula, often scattered among the vineyards. Regional differences in climate, terrain, and soil, as well as production and storage methods, all influence the character and complexity of the oils. Some are richly flavored, fruity, and peppery; others are delicate and refined. Tuscan oils have enjoyed the reputation for being "the best," with Umbrian oils a close second, but many regions produce great oils. The best oil is designated *olio extravergine*—extra virgin olive oil—and the finest are stone-ground and cold-pressed so that heat cannot compromise the flavor. The regions of Abruzzi, Apulia, Campania, Emilia-Romagna, Friuli–Venezia Giulia, Lazio, Le Marche, Liguria, the Molise, Sardegna, Sicilia, Toscana, Trentino, Umbria, and Veneto all produce olive oils, each with its own characteristics. (See Market Buying Tips: *Olio d'oliva*.)

Oliva (oh LEE vah). Olive.

Olive ripiene (oh LEE veh ree PYAY neh). This is a delicious antipasto from Le Marche, but it appears in other regions as well. The excellent local large green olives are pitted, stuffed with a mixture of meat and Parmesan, then deep-fried. Definitely worth trying!

Orecchiette (oh reh KYET teh). A type of pasta. (See *Pasta* below.)

Origano (oh ree GAH noh). Oregano.

Orzo (OR zoh). Barley.

Osei (OH zay). Game birds.

Osso buco (AWS soh BOO koh). Literally, "bone with a hole." A Milanese dish of braised veal shanks, slow-cooked with onion, carrot, celery, tomatoes, broth, and wine. Traditionally, it's topped with a pungent *gremolada* (grem oh LAH dah), a mixture of minced fresh parsley, garlic, and lemon peel.

Ostriche (aws TREE kay). Oysters.

Pancetta (pahn CHET tah). This is the fabulous, salt-cured bacon (unsmoked, except in Italy's northern-most regions) that has a delicious, mild flavor and is used to flavor innumerable dishes.

Pane (PAH nay). Bread. It varies widely, often according to region, but the basic bread is white or whole wheat with a (we hope) crisp crust. The saltless bread of Toscana is often considered tasteless by those not accustomed to it, but it pairs beautifully with the highly spiced *salumi* of the region. Rolls, called *panini* (pah NEE nee), are common, as are the *rosette*, or "little roses," that are all crust and hollow. (See *Bruschetta, Carta da musica, Fettunta, Focaccia,* and *Grissini* above, and *Schiacciata* below, and Regional/Seasonal Specialties: Puglia: *Pane* and Market Buying Tips: *Pane*.)

Panettone (pah neht TOH neh). A sweet yeast cake from Milano made with raisins, candied citron, orange, and eggs. It's a Christmas tradition that has traveled well beyond the confines of Lombardia and the season. (See Regional/Seasonal Specialties: Lombardia: Introduction and Market Buying Tips: *Panettone*.)

Panino (pah NEE noh). Sandwich.

Panna (PAHN nah). Cream.

Panna cotta (PAHN nah KOT tah). Literally, "cooked cream." A rich, creamy dessert from Piemonte. (See Regional/Seasonal Specialties: Piemonte: *Panna cotta*.)

Panna montata (PAHN nah mohn TAH tah). Whipped cream.

Panzanella (pahn tzah NEL lah). Bread salad that consists of mixed vegetables, including tomatoes, cucumbers, onion, and fresh basil, with cubes of stale bread that are briefly soaked in water and "refreshed" with olive oil. One of the many ingenious methods for using up yesterday's bread. It's a dish typical of Toscana.

Pappa col pomodoro (PAHP pah kol pom oh DAW roh). This Tuscan-style tomato soup utilizes yesterday's stale bread for thickening, a common strategy in that region. It's flavored with garlic and basil and enriched with olive oil.

Pappardelle (pah pahr DEHL lay). A type of pasta. (See *Pasta* below.)

Parmigiano-reggiano (pahr mee GYA noh reh JAH noh). The Parmesan that's constantly imitated but has never been duplicated. A world-class product of Emilia-Romagna that many revere as the finest cheese in the world. It comes from the area northwest of Bologna, and can be made only from the milk of cows that graze on the land of Parma, Reggio Emilia, and portions of three other provinces. It's most often used as a grating cheese over pasta or folded into risotto or polenta, but the exquisite, nutty flavor pairs magnificently with wines, especially rich, heady reds. Very strict rules govern the making of this cheese. For instance, a portion of whole milk, obtained that very morning, mixed with partially skimmed milk from the evening before, must be used. The cheese is aged for approximately two years. (See Regional/Seasonal Specialties: Emilia-Romagna: Introduction and Market Buying Tips: *Formaggi: Parmigiano-reggiano*.)

Pasta (PAH stah). Noodles in all their myriad forms, but the word can also refer to a pastry, *una pasta*. There are two basic categories: dried, factory-made pasta of flour and water and homemade, or *fresh*, pasta, made with egg and flour. Neither is superior, they are simply different, and lend themselves to different types of sauces and preparations. Whether or not Italy is the originator of pasta, she certainly has run with the concept! *Pasta asciutta* (ah SHYOOT tah) literally means "dry" but actually indicates pasta that is served with a sauce, as opposed to *pasta in brodo* (een BRAW doh), which is pasta cooked and served in broth. Following is a list of the more common forms of pasta and sauces that can adorn them.

Pasta

- *Agnolotti* (ahn yoh LOH tee). Round, meat-stuffed fresh pasta.
- *Bigoli* (bee GOH lee). A whole-wheat spaghetti-like pasta that's a specialty of Veneto. (See Regional/Seasonal Specialties: Veneto: *Bigoli*.)
- *Bucatini* (boo kah TEE nee). Thick, hollow spaghetti-like strands that are more common in the southern regions.
- *Cannelloni* (kahn nayl LOH nee). In northern Italy, these are meat-stuffed pasta cylinders, often handmade, topped first with meat sauce, then with a thin béchamel sauce. In the south, these pasta shells could be stuffed with fish.
- *Capelli d'angelo* (kah PEYL lee D'AHN jay loh). Angel-hair pasta. Very thin noodles.
- *Cappelletti* (kahp pel LET tee). These handmade, filled pastas of Romagna are shaped like a cap. They are called tortellini in Bologna.
- *Cappellini* (kahp pel LEE nee). Long, very thin strands of pasta.
- *Chitarre* (kee TAHR ray). Narrow, square-sided noodles made in Abruzzo.

- *Conchiglie* (kon KEEL yeh). Shell-shaped dried pasta.
- *Farfalle* (far FAHL leh). Bow-tie-shaped pasta.
- *Fettuccine* (fet too CHEE nee). A flat noodle, about three-eighths of an inch wide, often made fresh in Italy. (See Comfort Foods: Pasta and Regional/Seasonal Specialties: Lazio: *Pasta: Fettuccine maestose al burro*.)
- *Fusilli* (foo ZEE lee). Corkscrew-shaped dried pasta.
- *Gnocchi* (NYOH kee). The fabulous small dumplings made of boiled mashed potato, semolina, or rice mixed with flour. The particular ingredients and the sauces vary according to region.
- *Lasagne* (lah ZAHN yay). The wide, flat noodle we've all come to love. (See Comfort Foods: Pasta.)
- *Linguine* (leen GWEE nay). Narrow, flat noodles. (See Comfort Foods: Pasta.)
- *Maccheroni* (mahk keh ROH nee). The short, hollow tubular pasta. (See Comfort Foods: Pasta.)
- *Manfrigoli* (mahn free GOH lee). This spectacular, rustic, homemade pasta from Umbria is made with the grain emmer, or *farro*, and generally sauced with tomatoes and garlic. It is also known as *stringozzi* (streen GOHT tsee). (See Regional/Seasonal Specialties: Umbria: *Pasta.*)
- *Manicotti* (mah nee KOHT tee). The familiar cylinders of pasta that are stuffed with ricotta and meat, topped with tomato sauce, and oven-baked.

- *Orecchiette* (oh rek KYET teh). Pasta shaped like an ear.
- *Pappardelle* (pahp pahr DEHL lay). A Bolognese specialty, these are wide, homemade, hand-cut ribbons of pasta that measure almost one inch wide and six inches long. They are usually served with rich meat sauces. (See Regional/Seasonal Specialties: *Pasta:* Emilia-Romagna *Pappardelle* and Toscana *Pappardelle*.)
- *Pasticcio* (pahs TEE chyoh). The word means "pie," but when it's listed under pasta, it's an oven-baked, layered pasta dish similar to lasagne.
- *Penne* (PEYN nay). This short, hollow, tubular-shaped pasta is rather quill-shaped.
- *Pici* (PEE chee). This highly revered, hand-rolled spaghetti from Toscana is worth seeking out when you're in the area.
- *Ravioli* (rah VYOH lee). These well-known, square pastas are filled with various stuffings, either meat or a combination of meat, cheese, and/or vegetables, and topped with various sauces.
- *Rigatoni* (ree gah TOH nee). The large-diameter, tubular, hollow pasta is a popular form of macaroni.
- *Spaghetti/spaghettini* (spah GET tee /spah get TEE nee). No surprises here! Long, rounded solid-core pasta. Spaghettini are the same shape but thinner. (See Comfort Foods: Pasta.)
- *Stringozzi*. (See *Pasta: Manfrigoli*.)
- *Tagliarini* (tahl yah REE nee). Ribbonlike egg

pasta cut one-sixteenth of an inch wide and served in soups or with light, delicate sauces.

- *Tagliatelle* (tahl yah TEL lay). These flat strips of (usually) handmade egg pasta from Emilia-Romagna are found on every menu in the region, often sauced with *ragù*, or meat sauce. (See Regional/Seasonal Specialties: Emilia-Romagna: *Pasta: Tagliatelle*.)
- *Tortelli* (tor TEL lee). This is the name for stuffed pasta from Emilia. The fillings vary widely. (See Regional/Seasonal Specialties: Emilia-Romagna: *Pasta: Tortelli*.)
- *Tortellini* (tor tel LEE nee). This ethereal hand-made, stuffed pasta of Bologna is most often filled with meats and Parmesan and served in a meat sauce. (See *Bolognese* sauce below and Regional/Seasonal Specialties: Emilia-Romagna: *Tortellini*.)
- *Tortelloni* (tor tel LOH nee). Stuffed pasta from Bologna that are similarly filled but larger than tortellini. (See Regional/Seasonal Specialties: Emilia-Romagna: *Pasta: Tortelloni*.)
- *Ziti* (TSEE tee). Short, narrow tubes of dried pasta.

Pasta/Salse (SAHL seh): Sauces

- *alla abruzzese* (ah broo TSAY zay). Abruzzo style, with a sauce of oil, garlic, and hot peppers.
- *con aglio e olio* (AL yoh ay OL yoh). The classic sauce of garlic cooked briefly in olive oil is an example of the *cucina povera*, the food of the poor,

inexpensive but full-flavored and delicious. The pasta is commonly topped with parsley and Parmesan.

- *all'amatriciana* (ahl ah mah tree CHYAH nah). A pasta sauce from Amatrice in the province of Lazio. Two versions exist. The older one, *bianca* (BYAHN kah), is also known as *alla gricia* (GREE chyah), and it dates back to the times before Columbus brought the tomato to Italy from the New World. It consists of either the Italian unsmoked bacon *pancetta* (pahn CHET tah), or *guanciale* (gwan CHAH lay), cured hog's jowl, along with *pecorino romano*, black (or sometimes red) pepper, and olive oil. The new version, *rossa* (ROS sah), includes tomatoes. The pasta used is *bucatini* (boo kah TEE nee) or *perciatelli* (peyr chah TEL lee), a thick, hollow spaghetti. (See Regional/Seasonal Specialties: Lazio: *Pasta: Bucatini all'amatriciana*.)

- *all'arrabbiata* (ahr rahb BYAH tah). The translation is "angry" sauce, and the name is derived from the obligatory hot red pepper. The sauce also contains tomato and can include sausage or bacon.

- *alla bolognese* (boh lohn NYAY zeh). Also called *ragù* (rah GOO) or *al sugo* (SOO goh) is the rich meat sauce of Bologna, often containing several types of browned chopped meats (beef, pork, veal, sausage), braised vegetables such as carrots, celery, onion, and sometimes tomatoes, slow-cooked with water or stock, wine, and even cream.

- *in brodo* (BRAW doh). In broth.
- *al burro* (BOOR roh). The term indicates the use of fresh butter, usually with the addition of Parmesan.
- *alla cacciatora* (kaht chah TOH rah). "Hunter's-style" dishes vary according to the "hunter," but they usually include meat, tomatoes, mushrooms, and white wine.
- *alla carbonara* (kahr boh NAH rah). Hot cooked pasta (usually spaghetti) is tossed with sautéed garlic and pancetta (unsmoked bacon), then mixed with raw egg (in theory, the heat of the pasta cooks the egg), parmigiano, pecorino Romano, and black pepper. (See Regional/Seasonal Specialties: Lazio: *Pasta: Spaghetti alla carbonara*.)
- *alla casa* (KAH sah), or *casalinga* (KAH sah LEEN gah). "House style," which varies according to the restaurant but is usually a tomato-based sauce with meat and herbs.
- *alla contadina* (kon tah DEE nah). This is peasant or rustic-style sauce often based on butter, as opposed to oil, with mushrooms, onion, tomatoes, herbs, and Parmesan.
- *alla cozze* (KOH tsay). A southern Italian dish with mussels, garlic, olive oil, parsley, and sometimes tomatoes.
- *al forno* (FOR noh). Pasta dishes that are baked in the oven such as lasagne and manicotti.
- *ai frutti di mare* (FROOT tee dee MAH ray). This is an olive oil–based sauce with various seafoods and fresh herbs.

- *alla marinara.* (See Comfort Foods: Pasta: *Marinara, alla.*)
- *alla Norma* (NOR mah). A delicious sauce, named after Vincenzo Bellini's opera *Norma*. It contains eggplant, tomatoes, basil, and cheese.
- *al pesto* (PEY stoh). The area around Genoa boasts the finest basil, which, of course, yields the very best pesto. The classic preparation contains coarsely ground basil leaves, garlic, pine nuts, olive oil, and pecorino and Parmesan.
- *alla piemontese* (pyey mohn TAY zay). "In the style of Piedmont" usually means the pasta is topped with meat sauce, butter, nutmeg, and a garnish of thinly sliced white truffles—*tartufi* (tahr TOO fee). Truffles are sold by weight. They are weighed before slicing and after, and you are charged—handsomely—according to the number of grams you have allowed the waiter to shave onto your dish.
- *al pomodoro* (pom oh DAW roh). A simple olive oil–based tomato sauce cooked with onion, garlic, and herbs. (See Comfort Foods: Pasta: *Pasta al pomodoro.*)
- *alla puttanesca* (poo tahn ES kah). "Harlot's style." Contains olive oil, garlic, anchovies, capers, and olives, all staples in the kitchen. This dish could be whipped up quickly by ladies of ill repute between "tricks"!
- *al ragù* (rah GOO). In meat sauce, or *al ragù bolognese.* It's the genuine, slow-cooked sauce of

Bologna, made with pork, beef, carrots, celery, onion, tomatoes, wine, milk, and cream.

- *Ripiena* (ree PYAY nah). The word means "stuffed" or "filled," and it refers to stuffed pastas such as ravioli and tortellini.
- *alla romagnola* (roh mahn NYOH lah). A fresh tomato sauce.
- *alla romana* (roh MAH nah). Roman-style, denoting a seasoned meat sauce with grated Parmesan.
- *con le sarde* (kon leh SAHR deh). Pasta with sardines, pine nuts, anchovies, and raisins, representative of the *agrodolce,* or sweet/sour, tradition of Sicilia.
- *al tonno* (TON noh). Pasta with tuna. It's an olive oil–based sauce made with canned (not fresh) tuna, garlic, tomatoes, capers, and parsley.

Pasta e fagioli (PAH stah ay fah JOH lee). A hearty soup made with pasta and dried beans that appears in many regions of Italy. One excellent sample is from Toscana, where you can expect it to include *cannellini,* garlic, pancetta, carrots, celery, onion, chicken broth, and pasta, of course. It's usually flavored with rosemary or sage and always enriched with a dollop of the wonderful green-tinged Tuscan olive oil, which invariably graces your table. In Veneto, the marbled pink and white cranberry bean is used, along with onion, carrots, celery, tomatoes, broth, often a pork bone, and pasta. Another delicious version comes from Campania. This is comfort food, Italian-style.

Pasta reale (PAH stah reh YAH leh). Marzipan or almond paste. (See Regional/Seasonal Specialties: Sicilia: *Pasta reale.*)

Pastiera (pahs TYAY rah). Napoli's traditional Easter cake consists of a base of dough, a ricotta filling studded with candied fruit, and a topping of strips of dough formed into a lattice.

Patata (pah TAH tah). Potato.

Pecorino (peh koh REE noh). Cheese made from sheep's milk, which can be fresh or aged. When it's fresh, the cheese is soft and creamy, but as it ages, it becomes hard and suitable for grating. In springtime, freshly made *pecorino fresco* (peh koh REE noh FRAY skoh), sometimes called *marzolino* (mahr tzo LEE noh), is often paired with fresh, raw fava beans. Another ethereal pairing is that of aged pecorino with pears. The sharper-tasting aged pecorino produced in the southern regions of Sardegna and Lazio *(pecorino romano)* is especially good when grated over the spicy pasta dishes of the south. (See Regional/Seasonal Specialties: Abruzzo: *Formaggio di pecora*, Lazio: Introduction, and Sardegna: Introduction, and Market Buying Tips: *Formaggi: Pecorino.*)

Penne. (PAY nay). A type of pasta. (See *Pasta* above.)

Pepe nero (PEY peh NEY roh). Black pepper.

Peperonata (peh peh roh NAH tah). Mixed sweet peppers that are cooked and used as a side dish or as a topping for pasta, common in most of the southern regions, especially Campania.

Peperoncini (pey pey rohn CHEE nee). Devilishly hot red peppers that are used extensively in southern Italian savory dishes.

Peperoni (pey pey ROH nee). The word for sweet bell peppers, *not* the little rounds of spicy sausage found on pizzas in America.

Pera (PEY rah). Pear.

Pescatora, alla (pey skah TOH rah). The term indicates a dish containing fish and seafood.

Pesce (PAY shay). Fish. Both freshwater and saltwater fish and seafood are widely enjoyed by the Italians. You'll see many unfamiliar local varieties, both in Italian markets and listed on menus, but they are generally extremely fresh, very simply prepared, and well worth trying. Almost all come from the surrounding seas or freshwater lakes and rivers. The main exception is the dried salt cod, or *baccalà* (bah kah LAH), which is now imported from Norway. In its dried state, *baccalà* is most unappealing, but, reconstituted and cooked properly, it can be delicious. By the way, with *rare* exceptions, Italians don't top their fish and seafood dishes with cheese!

Pesce spada (PAY shay SPAH dah). Swordfish, a favorite catch from the waters surrounding Calabria and Sicilia. Often it's marinated with olive oil and fresh herbs such as oregano, then grilled, but other more involved dishes are made as well, such as *al pomodoro, olive e uvetta* (ahl pom oh DAW roh, oh LEE veh ay oo VET tah), a Sicilian preparation with a sauce of tomatoes, olives, raisins, capers, fresh herbs, onion, and garlic.

Pesche (PES kay). Peaches.

Pesto (PEY stoh). The pungent green sauce that's made such an impact on this side of the Atlantic. The classic, which originated in Genoa, is made with fresh basil leaves, pine nuts, garlic, pecorino and parmigiano cheeses, and olive oil. (See *Basilico* and *Pasta/Salse: al pesto* above and Regional/Seasonal Specialties: Liguria: *Pesto*.)

Petto (PEYT toh). Breast. On the menu it refers to the breast of chicken, duck, goose, or turkey.

Piadina (pyah DEE nah). The flatbread of Romagna. (See Regional/Seasonal Specialties: Emilia-Romagna: *Piadina*.)

Piccante (peek KAHN tay). Spicy, or sharp-flavored.

Piccata (peek KAH tah). Thin slice of meat (usually veal or chicken), cooked in butter and lemon juice.

Piccione (peet CHOH nay). Squab or pigeon.

Pignoli (pee NYOH lee). Pine nuts.

Pinzimonio (peen tse MOH nyoh). Assorted raw vegetables (crudités, actually), dipped in olive oil.

Piselli (pee SEL lee). Peas.

Pizzaiola, alla (peet tzah YOH lah). This term indicates a dish topped with an olive oil–based sauce of garlic, tomatoes, and oregano.

Polenta (poh LEHN tah). Cornmeal. Corn was unknown in Italy before explorations of the New World, but cornmeal replaced the other cereals of chickpea, millet, and buckwheat when it arrived at the port of Venezia in the early sixteenth century. It soon became an integral part of the diet of the poor. (Spaghetti and other factory-made pastas were not introduced to this region until northern industry began to attract laborers from the south.) Cornmeal, cooked in water with salt to a creamy and thick consistency, became the staple in northern Italy, sustaining life when little else was available. It was cooked the old-fashioned way, in a huge copper kettle suspended over the hearth. The cook would stir the mixture unceasingly for thirty to forty-five minutes, then pour the polenta onto a large wooden board. Dinner was served! Polenta has now become a trendy item and can be found on many menus, often topped with mushrooms or enriched with butter and grated fontina, parmigiano, or gorgonzola or as a bed for sauced meats, game birds, vegetables such as mushrooms, or seafood. It can also be chilled, sliced, then fried or grilled, to be served as a side dish or even made into desserts such as the cornmeal cake, often found in *trattorie* and *pasticcere*. (See Regional/Seasonal Specialties: Veneto: *Polenta e osei*.)

Pollastro (pol LAHS troh). Chicken. (See *Pollo* below.)

Pollo (POL loh). This is the most common word for chicken; other names include *gallina* (gahl LEE nah) and *pollastro* (pol LAHS troh). Most Italian menus will offer some fowl dish, whether it's chicken, capon—*cappone* (kahp POH neh), duck—*anatra* (AH nah tra), guinea fowl—*faraona* (fahr AH OH nah), or squab—*piccione* (peet CHOH nay).

• *Bollito* (bol LEE toh). Indicates that the chicken is "boiled," actually poached. It can be served with any number of sauces. "Boiled" chicken can also be listed as *lesso* (LES soh) or *lessato* (les SAHT toh).

- *Bietole, con* (KON BYEH toh leh). Chicken simmered in a vegetable broth with Swiss chard, then served on a bed of the chard.
- *Casalinga, alla* (kah sah LEEN gah). "Home-style." Indicates the recipe is at the whim of the house.
- *Crocchette di pollo* (kroh KET teh). Fried chicken croquettes.
- *Diavola, alla* (dee AH voh lah). Chicken that's "hot as the devil," made fiery with coarsely crushed red or black peppercorns.
- *Fritto alla fiorentina* (FREET toh ah lah fyor en TEE nah). Fried chicken, Florentine-style, which can be marinated with lemon and herbs and fried in olive oil or breaded and fried.
- *Indiana, all'* (een DYAHN ah). "In the style of India" is curried chicken.
- *Insalata di pollo* (een sah LAH tah). Chicken salad, a marvelous specialty of Piemonte, where it's dressed with olive oil, lemon juice, and white truffles.
- *Mattone, al* (maht TOH neh). One of the preparations that is now being presented by chefs on this side of the ocean is literally chicken cooked "under bricks." This is actually a chicken, split and cooked whole, pressed down to the skillet (or the grill) with a weight (traditionally bricks) to fry. Kitchenware shops carry special two-piece glazed pottery cookers with heavy, flat tops made for this purpose. The method produces a delicious, crisp, nongreasy crust.
- *Pollastro in tecia* (pol LAHS troh een TAY chah). A

classic chicken dish of Veneto cooked with onions and cloves and served with polenta.

- *Porchetta* (pore KET tah). Indicates chicken cooked in the manner of a suckling pig, that is, in a wood-burning oven, flavored with garlic, rosemary, fennel, and mint. And *pollo alla romana* (ro MAH nah) is a beautiful dish served mainly in summer in Rome. It's flavored with garlic, prosciutto (pro SHOOT toh), tomatoes, and colorful bell peppers. (See Comfort Foods: Chicken.)

Polpette (pohl PET teh). Meatballs, frequently pan-fried and served as part of the *secondo piatto*. They are made with a variety of meats, often a combination of two or more such as beef, along with some chicken and a little flavoring from pork. When listed as *d'agnello* (dahn YEL loh), the meatballs are made with ground lamb, often seasoned with wild mint, as well as the usual onion and garlic. These are especially popular in the southern regions. When listed as *all'agrodolce* (ahl ahg roh DOL chay), they're sweet and sour meatballs, cooked with raisins, sugar, and wine vinegar, a legacy of the ancient Arabic invasions of southern Italy. (See Comfort Foods: Meatballs and Regional/Seasonal Specialties: Sardegna: *Polpette d'agnello*.)

Polpettone (pohl peht TOH neh). Meat loaf, often made with ground veal and commonly flavored with ham, cheese, and fresh herbs.

Polpo (POL poh). Octopus. *Polpetielli* (pol peh TYEL lee) are tiny baby octopuses.

Pomodoro (pom oh DAW roh). Tomato. It's hard to imagine, but the tomato was unknown in Italy before Columbus brought it back from the New World! Now the tomato is synonymous with Italian cooking, whether fresh, in a sauce, or dried in the sun. You might have guessed that each region has its own favorite variety, from the plum to the much revered *san marzano,* which is used extensively for sauces because of its meaty pulp.

Pompelmo (pom PEHL moh). Grapefruit.

Porchetta (por KET tah). Roast suckling pig. *In porchetta* (een por KET tah) refers to the method of cooking, stuffed and baked in a wood-burning oven, in the same manner as the suckling pig. (See *Carpa, Maiale,* and *Pollo* above and Regional/Seasonal Specialties: Lazio: *Porchetta,* Le Marche: *Coniglio,* and Umbria: *Regina in porchetta.*)

Porcini (por CHEE nee). These are the huge, meaty mushrooms, named after "little pigs" in Italian, that are found over much of Italy. In their fresh state, they can be grilled like a steak, eaten raw, marinated in wine vinegar and olive oil, or sautéed with garlic. In their dried form, porcini appear in sauces, pastas, and rice dishes throughout the year. (See Regional/

Seasonal Specialties: Calabria: *Porcini* and Market Buying Tips: *Funghi.*)

Prezzemolo (pret tsay MOH loh). Parsley.

Prosciutto (pro SHOOT toh). Ham. *Affumicato* (ah foo mee KAH toh) refers to raw ham that's been cured and wood-smoked. *Cotto* (KOT toh) means cooked (actually boiled) ham. *Prosciutto crudo* (pro SHOOT toh KROO doh) literally means "raw," but the term refers to salted, air-cured ham. It's also known as *prosciutto di parma,* probably the best known of the cured hams, from the regions surrounding Parma in Emilia-Romagna. *Prosciutto crudo di San Daniele* (sahn dahn YEH leh) is Friuli's outstanding cured ham, famous since medieval times, that rivals *prosciutto di Parma.* (See Regional/ Seasonal Specialties: Emilia-Romagna: *Prosciutto* and Umbria: *Prosciutto di cinghiale* and Market Buying Tips: *Salumi.*)

Provolone (pro voh LOH neh). One of Italy's most famous cheeses, served both fresh, when it's more delicate in flavor, and aged, when its flavor is more pronounced.

Quaglia (KWAH lyah). Quail. (See Regional/Seasonal Specialties: Le Marche: *Quaglie in umido.*)

Quattro formaggi (KWAHT roh for MAHD jee). Literally, "four cheeses." Refers to preparations using four types of cheese. They can vary, but Emmenthal, fontina, Gruyère, and parmigiano are commonly used together.

Radicchio (rah DEE kyoh). The slightly bitter-tasting red-leaf lettuce, served raw in salads and also grilled or oven-roasted. (See Regional/Seasonal Specialties: Veneto: *Radicchio.*)

Ragù (rah GOO). This is a general term for sauces made from any variety of chopped meats, sautéed vegetables, and one or more liquids, such as water, stock, wine, tomato, milk, or cream. These sauces are made throughout Italy, but they are especially well known in Emilia-Romagna. (See *Pasta/Salse: alla bolognese* and *al ragù* above and Regional/Seasonal Specialties: Emilia-Romagna: *Pasta: Ragù.*)

Ravioli (Rah VYOH lee). A type of pasta. (See *Pasta* above.)

Ribollita (ree bohl LEE tah). Literally, "reboiled," this thick soup is made of vegetables, stale bread, and olive oil, and is reheated the following day.

Ricotta (ree KOH tah). Literally, "cooked again." It's the soft, fresh white cheese made from whey, a by-product of cheese making. The thrifty cheese makers heat the whey a second time, creating the delightful, mild cheese that's used in both savory and sweet dishes. The cheese is made with slight variations in almost all the regions, with milk from either cows or sheep. *Ricotta salata* (ree KOHT tah sah LAH tah) is a firmer, salted cheese. (See Regional/Seasonal Specialties: Puglia: Introduction and Market Buying Tips: *Formaggi: Ricotta*.)

Rigatoni (ree gah TOH nee). A type of pasta. (See *Pasta* above.)

Ripieni (ree PYAY nee). The term indicates any item that is filled or stuffed, such as pastas (ravioli, cannelloni) or vegetables like onions, zucchini, and eggplant, which can be stuffed, baked, and served as antipasti or side dishes.

Ris e fasui (REEZ ay FAHS wee). Rice, bean, and potato soup of the northern region of Friuli–Venezia Giulia. Perfect for the starch lover!

Risi e bisi (REE zee ay BEE see). Rice with fresh young peas that originated in Venice. (See Regional/Seasonal Specialties: Veneto: *Risi e bisi*.)

Riso (REE zoh). Rice. Although pasta is king in Italy, Italians eat plenty of rice, mainly in the form of risotto, most commonly as a *primo*, or first course.

Risotto (ree ZOHT toh). A sensational, creamy rice dish, served as a first course and made with a very starchy rice (often the superfino variety) that is grown predominantly on the plains surrounding the Po River. Other types, such as *Vialone Nano* and *Carnaroli*: are grown in Piemonte, Veneto, and Lombardia. Originating in the north, risotto can now be found throughout the peninsula, as well as in the United States. The classic cooking method begins with toasting the rice in a pan with butter. Hot broth is added in increments until the grains are cooked *al dente* and the mixture is creamy. Butter and *parmigiano* are then added with a flourish. The result should be creamy and slightly liquid—*not* sticky. The variations are endless, varying according to the indigenous ingredients of each region and to the season. *Risotto alla milanese* from Lombardia is made with the addition of saffron, *zafferano* (zahf fay RAH noh). Springtime versions appear in Rome with baby artichokes and peas, *carciofi e piselli* (kahr CHOH fee ay pee SEL lee). The hearty, rose-colored risotto from Piemonte, flavored with a *barolo* (bah ROH loh), sustains the diner on a cold winter's night. (See Regional/Seasonal Specialties: Lombardia: Introduction and *Risotto alla milanese*, Piemonte: *Panissa*, Veneto: Introduction and *Risotto*, and Market Buying Tips: *Riso*.)

Rosmarino (rawz mah REE noh). Rosemary.

Rospo (ROS poh). Monkfish, sometimes known as "poor man's lobster" because when cooked its texture is similar to that of lobster tail. *Coda di rospo* (KOH dah dee ROS poh) means "tail of monkfish," which is the portion that is consumed. This fish, prepared several ways, is especially popular in Venice.

Rosso (ROS soh). Red.

Rucola (roo KOH lah). Arugula, the delicious, rocket-shaped, sharp-flavored green currently adored by foodies. You'll often find it in mixed green salads.

Salame (sal LAH meh). This is salt-cured pork sausage, found throughout Italy. (See Market Buying Tips: *Salumi*.)

Salmone (sahl MOH nay). Salmon, which can be fresh or smoked.

Salsiccia (sahl SEET chah). Sausage, which in Italy is most often made from pork. Spicy pork sausage, pervasive throughout Italy, can be found in a variety of dishes. Most often it is cooked in a casserole with legumes or potatoes or atop pizza. (See *Norcina* above and Regional/Seasonal Specialties: Abruzzo: *Salsicce di fegato*, Friuli–Venezia Giulia: *Polenta e salsiccia*, and Umbria: *Salsiccia di cinghiale*.)

Saltimbocca (sahl teem BOK kah). Literally, "jump in the mouth," with the inference of irresistibility. (See Regional/Seasonal Specialties: Lazio: *Saltimbocca alla romana*.)

Salumi (sah LOO mee). A general term referring to cold cuts such as salami and prosciutto (pro SHOOT toh). Each region makes its own version(s), and each claims to have "the best." (See *Capocollo, Cotechino, Prosciutto,* and *Salame* above, *Soppressata* below, Regional/Seasonal Specialties: Emilia-Romagna: *Coppa, Cotechino, Culatello,* and *Mortadella,* Friuli–Venezia Giulia: *Musett,* Lombardia: *Bresaola,* Puglia: Introduction, and Market Buying Tips: *Salumi.*)

Salvia (SAHL vyah). Sage.

San Pietro (sahn pee AYT roh). St. Peter's fish, also known as John Dory, is found along rocky coastlines. It has delicious, firm, white flesh that's very versatile; it can be grilled, braised, sautéed, or used in fish soups.

Sarde (SAHR deh). Sardines. (See Regional/Seasonal Specialties: Le Marche: *Sarde alla marchigiana.*)

Scaloppine (skah loh PEE ney). This refers to a thin slice of meat (often veal) from the top round, pounded flat to cook quickly and evenly. The meat can be sauced in any number of ways. (See *Vitello* below.)

Scamorza (skah MORE zah). A firm-textured sheep's cheese of the southern regions, it's made in the shape of a pear and often served grilled, in which case it's listed variously as *allo spiedo* (ah loh SPYEH doh), *ai ferri* (ay FER ree), or *alla griglia* (ah lah GREEL yah).

Scampi (SKAHM pee). The Italian word for "shrimp." So if you order "shrimp scampi," you are really saying "shrimp shrimp." The usual connotation of scampi is of a large prawn. When the menu reads *all'Americana* (ahl ah mehr ee KAH nah) they will be simmered in tomato sauce, occasionally enriched with cream. *Fritti* (FREET tee) are fried shrimp, which are probably as popular in Italy as they are in America. They're usually floured, then deep-fried in light olive oil. *Spiedino di* (spyeh DEE noh) means they're skewered and cooked on a grill. One of the simplest preparations is *alla veneziana* (vay neetz YAH nah), done in the style of Venice, boiled and served with fresh lemon juice—a treat for the purist!

Scarola (skah ROH lah). Escarole, or curly endive.

Schiacciata (skyaht CHYAH tah). Flatbread. (See Comfort Foods: Pizza: *Foccacia* and Regional/Seasonal Specialties: Toscana: *Schiacciata al rosmarino* and Umbria: *Schiacciata*.)

Secco (SEHK koh). Dry.

Sedano (SEH dah noh). Celery.

Semi (SEH mee). Seeds.

Semifreddo (SEH mee FRAYD doh). Literally, "partially" or "half frozen," it's a delightful, smooth dessert, reminiscent of frozen mousse. *Semifreddo* is made with uncooked eggs and whipped cream and often flavored with chocolate or espresso. Note: Although reports of illness due to tainted eggs have not been reported in Italy, diners, especially those with compromised immune systems, should always be aware of the possibility of contamination and avoid dishes like this.

Seppie (SEP pyay). Technically, this is cuttlefish, but it often refers to its relative, the squid. When served *in tecia col nero* (een TEY chah kol NEY ro), a typical dish of Veneto, you will get a rich stew made black with the ink of the squid, served over polenta or risotto. The sauce can be thinned out and served over pasta as well.

Sfoglia (SFOH lyah). A sheet of homemade egg pasta, or pastry dough.

Sgombro (SGOHM broh). Mackerel.

Sogliola (soh LYOH lah). Sole, which is very highly prized for its fine-textured flesh. You'll often find it served *arrosto* (ah ROAS toh), when the whole fish is generally served, roasted in an herb-spiked olive oil and white wine. *Dorata* (doh RAH tah) means dusted with flour, dipped in egg and bread crumbs, then fried. You'll recognize *alla mugnaia* (moo NYA ya), better known as meunière, dusted with flour, fried in oil and butter, then flavored with parsley and lemon slices. And in Naples, it's often served *alla partenopea* (pahr teh no PEH ah), poached in fish stock and white wine, served over tubular pasta, and topped with cheese (unusual for fish) and a creamy white sauce.

Soppressata (soh preh SAH tah). This is a type of pork sausage or *salame* (sahl LAH meh) made in Toscana and most of the southern Italian regions, where it appears frequently on antipasti platters. (See Market Buying Tips: *Salumi.*)

Sorbetto (sor BEHT toh). Sorbet or sherbet.

Speck (SPEK). A product of Alto Adige. Cold-smoked ham marinated in brine with herbs and spices. (See Regional/Seasonal Specialties: Trentino–Alto Adige: *Speck* and Market Buying Tips: *Salumi.*)

Spezie (SPEH tzyeh). Spices.

Spiedo (SPYEH doh) or *Spiedino* (spyeh DEE noh). Skewer. Foods cooked *alla spiedo* are skewered and grilled.

Spugnoli (spoon NYOH lee). Morels (mushrooms).

Stimpirata (steem pee RAH tah). A flavorful preparation from Sicilia, usually applied to swordfish. Onions and celery are cooked in olive oil along with capers. The fish is floured and fried in another pan, then finished in the first pan, spiked with wine vinegar.

Stinco (STEEN koh). A Friulian traditional dish in which a whole veal shank is cooked Trieste-style, with onion and garlic, and slowly braised with white wine and anchovies.

Stracciatella (strah chah TEHL lah). The term can refer to soup as in *stracciatella alla romana* (strah chah TEHL lah ah lah ro MAH nah). In this case it's chicken broth to which eggs mixed with a little semolina (flour) and grated cheese are added at the last minute, then swirled "egg drop style" (kind of an Italian egg drop soup). If it's on the menu at a *gelateria*, *stracciatella* refers to chocolate chip *gelato*!

Stringozzi (streen GOH tsee). A type of pasta. (See *Pasta* above and Regional/Seasonal Specialties: Umbria: *Pasta: Stringozzi*.)

Succo di frutta (SOOK koh dee FROOT tah). Fruit juice.

Sugo (SOO goh). Sauce or gravy.

Surgelato (soor jay LAH toh). "Frozen." Italian menus must divulge the fact that certain foods (such as fish) or their ingredients have been frozen.

Tacchino (tahk KEE noh). Turkey. (See Regional/ Seasonal Specialties: Emilia-Romagna: *Tacchino al cardinale.*)

Tagliatelle (tahl yah TEL lay). A type of pasta. (See *Pasta* above.)

Taleggio (tah LEJ yoh). A wonderfully rich, ripe soft cheese from Lombardia. (See Regional/Seasonal Specialties: Lombardia: Introduction and Market Buying Tips: *Formaggi: Taleggio.*)

Tarocco (tah ROK koh). Blood orange, a fruit with bright-red flesh, can be a bit startling to see the first time. You might mistake its juice for tomato juice at first, but the flavor is that of orange juice.

Tartufi (tahr TOO fee). Truffles. They may be white, *bianco*, or black, *nero*. (See Regional/Seasonal Specialties: Piemonte: *Fonduta con tartufo* and *Tartufi*, Umbria: *Frittata di tartufi*, and Market Buying Tips: *Tartufi.*)

Timo (TEE moh). Thyme.

Tiramisù (tee rah mee SOO). One of the better-known desserts from Italy, similar to the English trifle. It contains the luscious triple-cream *mascarpone* (mahs kahr POH nay), wine or brandy, sponge cake, sugar, and espresso. The literal translation of "pick-me-up" originated with the espresso it contains.

Tonno (TOHN noh). This is tuna, which may be fresh or canned (in olive oil). Tuna is especially prevalent in the southern regions, where it's usually prepared simply so as not to detract from the flavor of the fresh fish. (See *Pasta / Salse: al tonno* above and Regional/Seasonal Specialties: Calabria: *Tonno alla calabrese,* Sicilia: *Tonno,* and Toscana: *Fagioli.*)

Torcolato (tor koh LAH toh). Sometimes called *serpentone,* it's a delicious coiled sweet roll (it looks like a coiled snake) from Umbria flavored with nuts and dried fruits.

Torta (TOR tah). Cake. It can be sweet or savory.

Tortellini (tor tel LEE nee). A type of pasta. (See Pasta above.)

Triglia (TREE lyay). Red mullet, a favorite fish from the waters surrounding Italy. It's often an essential ingredient in fish stews, especially along the Adriatic. (See Regional/Seasonal Specialties: Liguria: *Triglia alla genovese* and Puglia: *Triglia di scoglio.*)

Trippa (TREEP pah). Tripe is the stomach of those animals referred to as "ruminants," such as cows, sheep, and oxen. In these animals, the stomach is divided into four different parts. The "second stomach," which resembles honeycomb, is favored in Italy, where sheep tripe is the most common type. (See Regional/ Seasonal Specialties Abruzzo: *Trippa in umido,* Lombardia: *Busecca,* and Toscana: *Trippa alla fiorentina.*)

Trota (TROH tah). Trout. This highly prized fresh-water fish is a specialty in several regions. In Valle d'Aosta, it's served *al vino rosso* (ahl VEE noh ROS soh), cooked in red wine. In Trentino–Alto Adige, the fish is simmered in white wine vinegar, wine, and fresh herbs, a preparation known as *trota in blu* (TROH tah een BLOO). In Umbria, trout is usually prepared by grilling, perhaps with some herbs and a little olive oil. A delicious variation is *con l'agliata* (kon lah LYAH tah), in which the fish is covered with garlic paste that's made by mixing garlic with bread crumbs, a little water, lemon juice, and olive oil. Often the whole trout is grilled or broiled, then topped with the garlic paste.

Umido, in (OO mee doh). Poached. A very popular way of preparing almost any meat or game. The poaching liquid can vary from water to broth to wine and is often flavored with fresh herbs.

Uova (oo WO vah). Eggs.

Uva (OO vah). Grape.

Valdostana, alla (vahl dos TAH nah). In the style of Valle d'Aosta, a region in the northwest of Italy.

Vaniglia (vah NEEL yah). Vanilla.

Verdura (veyr DOO rah). The term generally refers to vegetables, although, literally, it means "greens."

Vitello (vee TEHL loh). Veal is one of the most popular meats in Italy.

- *Arrosto* (ah ROAS toh). Denotes a roast, often slow-cooked on the stove top (in the past, ovens were a rarity in most homes) with broth, wine, and various flavorings.
- *Battuta* (baht TOO tah). Can mean either that the meat was pounded or that it's minced or ground.
- *Bolognese, alla* (boh loh NYAY zay). Bologna-style; breaded, then fried in butter and covered with a slice of prosciutto and Parmesan that has been quickly melted in the oven. This is often topped with meat sauce. In another version, tomato sauce tops the meat, which is then baked.
- *Brace, alla* (BRAH chay). Indicates the meat was grilled over charcoal.
- *Ferri, ai* (FER ree). Literally means "on iron," but it means the veal was grilled.
- *Girello di vitello* (jee REHL loh). The round steak from the leg, which can be prepared in various ways: roasted, sliced and fried, sautéed, or braised.
- *Griglia, alla* (GREEL yah). Grilled.
- *Involtini* (een vohl TEE nee). Thin slices of veal, spread with various ingredients, sometimes ham and cheese, then rolled and braised in butter or

oil, flavored with wine or vinegar, and served with the pan sauce.

- *Lombata* (lom BAH tah). The loin, commonly served sautéed with ingredients such as mushrooms, herbs, and tomatoes.

- *Milanese, alla* (meel ahn AY zay). The classic from Milan, a bone-in veal chop, floured, dipped in beaten egg, then rolled in Parmesan and bread crumbs and fried in butter.

- *Osso buco* (AWS soh BOO koh). Veal shank, cut across the bone. It's slow-cooked with broth, wine, and often tomatoes or mushrooms, then traditionally topped with *gremolada* (grem oh LAH dah), a delicious combination of fresh lemon peel, minced garlic, and parsley. The bone marrow is a delicacy.

- *Panna, alla* (PAHN nah). Indicates your veal is fried in butter, then served in a sauce made with cream, lemon, and sometimes mushrooms.

- *Pizzaiola, alla* (peet tzah YOH lah). Consists of a slice of veal sautéed, then served with the pan sauce made with tomatoes, garlic, and oregano.

- *Scaloppine* (skah loh PEE nay). Indicates a boneless, thin slice of meat, and it can be prepared in an infinite number of ways.

- *Spezzatino di vitello* (speh tah TEE noh). A braised veal stew, generally cooked with tomatoes, broth, and fresh herbs.

- *Valdostana, alla* (vahl dos TAH nah). In the style of Valle d'Aosta includes a slice of fontina, either tucked inside a slit cut in the meat or placed over the top and melted. (See *Osso buco* above and *Vitello tonnato* below and Comfort Foods: Veal.)

Vitello tonnato (vee TEHL loh tohn NAH toh). This dish can serve as an elegant antipasto, a second course, or as part of a buffet. It consists of paper-thin slices of cooked veal smothered in a rich, smooth mayonnaise-based sauce that is made with tuna, anchovies, eggs, olive oil, lemon juice, and capers.

Vongole (VOHN goh leh). Clams, served especially in those regions bordering on the sea. *Reganate* (ray gah NAH teh) means they are steamed, then topped with garlic, bread crumbs, parsley, red pepper flakes, cheese, and olive oil and baked or broiled. Clams show up frequently in fish soups as well. (See *Zuppa di vongole* below and Comfort Foods: Pasta: Linguine with clam sauce and Pizza.)

Zabaione (zah bah YON eh), or *zabaglione*. An ethereal dessert made by whipping egg yolks with wine (usually Marsala [mahr SAH lah] but also *vin santo* [VEEN SAHN toh] or other dessert wines), and sugar, all of which are cooked over the flame until the mixture becomes frothy and has tripled in volume. It can be served warm or chilled, often with dry cookies or fresh fruit or as a sauce with a slice of cake.

Zafferano (zahf fay RAH noh). Saffron. (See *Risotto* above and Regional/Seasonal Specialties: Abruzzo: Introduction.)

Zampone (zahm POH nay). Pork sausage stuffed into a casing made from a pig's foot. (See Regional/Seasonal Specialties: Emilia-Romagna: *Zampone*.)

Zeppole (TSEP poh lay). These are dessert fritters, popular throughout southern Italy. They're served either plain, topped with confectioners' sugar, or garnished with rich pastry cream for feast days.

Ziti (TSEE tee). A type of pasta. (See *Pasta* above.)

Zucchero (TSOOK kay roh). Sugar.

Zuccotto (tsoo KOT toh). A dome-shaped dessert that's a Florentine specialty, consisting of a shell of pound cake, heavy cream, sugar, chocolate, almonds, hazelnuts, and a combination of liqueurs to soak the cake, including cognac, cherry-flavored maraschino, and an orange liqueur such as Cointreau.

Zuppa (TSOOP pah). Soup. (See *Minestra* above, *Zuppa di pesce*, *Zuppa inglese*, and *Zuppa di vongole* below, Comfort Foods: Soup, and Regional/Seasonal Specialties: Abruzzo: *Zuppa di scarola* and Valle d'Aosta: *Seuppa alla valdostana*, *Seupetta di cogne*, and *Zuppa do castagne*.)

Zuppa di pesce (TSOOP pah dee PAY shay). Also known as *brodetto*, a fish soup or stew, it's found all along the Adriatic coast. (See Comfort Foods: Soup and Regional/Seasonal Specialties: Basilicata: *Zuppa di pesce*.)

Zuppa di vongole (TSOOP pah dee VON goh lay). Clam soup that's usually comprised of onion, garlic, parsley, and tomatoes cooked with white wine and the local species of clams.

Zuppa inglese (TSOOP pah een GLAY say). Literally, "English soup," but it's actually a dessert. There are many versions of this impressive dish, but generally it consists of layers of sponge cake soaked with rum and layered with custard, jam, and chocolate—the Italian version of English trifle.

BEVERAGES A TO Z

· ▦ ·

THE LESS frenetic pace prevalent throughout most of Italy compared to that of the United States encourages both the native and the traveler to stop, have a drink, and soak up some of the local atmosphere. The *bar-caffè*, where both nonalcoholic and alcoholic drinks are available, is an excellent spot to partake in this ritual. Coffees, teas, mineral waters, and juices are on the menu, along with beer and before- and after-dinner drinks.

Rich, dark, and intensely flavored, *caffè* in Italy is more than a habit—it's an integral part of the day. In the morning, it's a quick demitasse of espresso gulped down at the bar or a steaming cup of *cappuccino* (kahp poo CHEE noh) or *caffè latte* (LAT tay) to accompany breakfast. Then there are the coffee stops at the *bar-caffè* during the day, not to mention the obligatory cup in the evening—after dessert, either at the restaurant or—you guessed it—back at the *bar-caffè*.

Mineral water will be offered when you order at

a restaurant. You'll be asked if you want carbonation, *gassata*, or *con gas*, or still, without gas, *naturale*. Italian tap water is safe to drink unless you see a sign saying *acqua non potabile* (NAWN po tah BEE leh). (Do keep in mind that safe water might still upset your system just because it is unfamiliar.)

The *enoteca* (ayn oh TEH kah) is a wineshop or bar. Most offer a chance to taste and enjoy a glass of wine, as well as the opportunity to purchase a bottle (or more). Some special *enotecas* have official duties, including disseminating information about Italian wines.

Before-dinner drinks are taken much more seriously in Italy than in America, so a stop for a predinner drink to stimulate the appetite is deemed prudent, if not downright therapeutic. As important as *aperitivi* (ah pair eh TEE vee) are before the meal, their importance pales in comparison to the *digestivi* (dee jes TEE vee) or *amari* (ah MAHR ee), the afterdinner drinks that also derive from varying herbs, barks, and roots. Many are extremely bitter, but Italy makes after-dinner liqueurs that are more palatable to Americans as well.

Restaurants rarely have a full bar, but they may serve a house cocktail—an *aperitivo della casa* (ah peh ree TEE voh deh lah KAH sah). It's usually a concoction of white wine mixed with some type of bitters. You can also get a glass of wine, or a wine, such as the slightly fizzy *spumante* (spoo MAHN tay), mixed with various flavors of fruit juice, *succo di frutta* (SOOK koh dee FROOT tah). Strong spirits such as whiskey and cognac are generally reserved for after the meal. You may have to ask for ice, *ghiaccio* (GYAHT choh). Italians don't like to dilute their drinks.

Acqua di soda (AH kwah dee SO dah). Soda water.

Acqua minerale (AH kwah mee neh RAH lay). Mineral water. It's a big business in Italy, in spite of the fact that today the country's tap water, *acqua del rubinetto* (roo bee NEHT toh), is safe to drink and, in some regions, is exceptionally good. There are more than 150 companies that bottle Italy's natural mineral water, and reading the labels can take you back to chemistry class. Long lists of the water's mineral content, including salt, and proof of bacteriological analysis and purity come under the heading of "more than you ever wanted to know." Here's what you do want to know: Is it artificially carbonated, *gassata* (gahs SAH tah), or still, *naturale* (nah too RAH leh). There is a third category—natural carbonation, called *frizzante* (free ZAHN teh). Italians seem to prefer some fizz. Mineral waters are thought to have therapeutic properties, and the supposed benefits (also listed on the label) are extensive. Taste a variety of waters to discover your personal favorite.

Aperitivi (ah peh ree TEE vee). Aperitifs. The menu will list several. Some will have immediate name recognition; many others will be unfamiliar.

- *Aperol* (ah PEYR ohl). Orange-flavored and frequently served in a glass whose rim is sugar-coated.
- *Campari* (kahm PAHR ree). Derived from quinine bark, herbs, and bitter orange peel, it will no doubt ring a bell. Distilled from a variety of fruits and vegetables, roots, herbs, and the bark of trees, its taste is often an acquired one.
- *Cinzano* (cheen TSAN oh). A well-known brand of vermouth. Both the red, rosso (ROS soh), and the white, bianco (bee AHN koh), are sweet. The drier versions are termed *secco* (SEHK koh).
- *Cynar* (CHEE nahr). A dark brown aperitif made from artichokes.
- *Limoncello* (lee mon CHAY loh). A lemon liqueur that's become a very popular *aperitivo*. It's made from the exquisite lemons grown on the Amalfi coast of Campania. The demand has grown to such an extent that imitations made with artificial ingredients are being produced. The label will confess this, so check it carefully.
- *Martini* (mahr TEE nee). Another brand of vermouth.
- *Negroni* (ney GROH nee). A cocktail that combines Campari with gin.
- *Punt e Mes* (poont ay MEYS). A brown bitter that's very popular in Italy.
- *Riccadonna* (reek kah DAWN nah). Another popular vermouth.

Aranciata (ah ran CHYAH tah). Orange soda.

Bellini (bel LEE nee). A cocktail created by Giuseppe Cipriani, the founder of the famous Harry's Bar in Venezia. It's made with Prosecco, a delicious, light, sparkling white wine from the region around Treviso, and peach puree, made from the incredible white peaches that grow in the Venetian lagoon. A definite don't-miss item in Venezia in the springtime.

Birra (BEER rah). Beer. It obviously takes a backseat to wine in Italy, but it is available, especially in the *bar-caffè*. The beers may be made in Italy—*nazionale* (nah tzee oh NAH lay), imported—*estera* (ES teh rah), or on draft—*alla spina* (SPEE nah). Some Italian beers you might want to try include Peroni and Peroni Extra, Nastro Azzuro, and Moretti.

Caffè (kah FAY). Coffee. It's hard to say just why the coffee in Italy is so exceptional, but it's obvious America has discovered the Italians' way with the bean from the veritable explosion of the Italian-inspired coffee industry here at home over the past few years. Words such as *cappuccino* and *latte* have become part of the vernacular, and we're acquainted with the rituals of coffeemaking and -drinking. But in case you haven't mastered quite all of the jargon, here's the scoop. The basics include:

• *Caffè* (kah FAY). Strong espresso served in a demitasse cup, not the weaker American coffee. If made properly, it will have delicious foam on top, called *crema* (KREH mah).

- *Caffè d'orzo* (DOR zoh). Ersatz coffee made from barley.
- *Cappuccino* (kahp poo CHEE noh). Translates literally as "the little hood" or "the little monk." The name refers to the color of the mixture, which resembles that of the Capuchin monk's robes. It's made with espresso and topped with foamy steamed milk. In Italy, it's mainly drunk in the morning, and never after a meal. Italians don't believe the milk sits well after a meal.
- *Corretto* (kor RET toh). Coffee that's been "corrected" with a shot of liquor.
- *Freddo* (FRED doh). Iced coffee.
- *Hag* (AHGH). Italy's brand-name decaffeinated coffee, but it's used as a generic term for decaf.
- *Latte* (LAT tay). Strong espresso mixed with a generous amount of hot milk, served in a large cup. *Caffè latte freddo* (kah FAY LAT tay FRED doh) is the chilled version.
- *Lungo* (LOON goh). Literally, "long," meaning coffee that's been brewed to be weaker, using more water.
- *Macchiato* (mah KYAH toh). Espresso "stained" with a small amount of hot milk.
- *Ristretto* (rees TRET toh). Coffee that's made stronger, using less water. (See Market Buying Tips: *Caffè*.)

Camomilla (kah moh MEEL lah). Camomile tea. It's caffeine-free and thought to be useful for relaxation and diuretic purposes.

Cioccolata calda (chee ohk koh LAH tah KAHL dah). Hot chocolate.

Crodino (kroh DEE noh) and *San Pellegrino* (SAHN peh leh GREE noh). Brand names of nonalcoholic carbonated bitters.

Digestivi (dee jes TEE vee). Digestives, or after-dinner drinks.

- *Acquavite* (AH kwah VEE teh). An after-dinner drink, similar to grappa, distilled from various fruits such as apples, pears, berries, and cherries. Like grappas, the best are produced in the northern regions.
- *Amaretto* (ah mah RET toh). A well-known after-dinner liqueur, redolent of almonds.
- *Amaro Lucano* (ah MAH roh loo KAH noh). A coffee-flavored *digestivo* (dee jes TEEF voh), or after-dinner drink, from the region of Abruzzo.
- *Fernet Branca* (fer NEHT BRAHN kah). The most bitter of all the digestives, but it is also regarded as the most effective, no doubt because it tastes the most medicinal. But consider yourself forewarned—this one is not for the faint of

heart. It is rumored to be habit-forming, but I can't imagine getting enough down to begin to form the habit!

- *Frangelico* (frahn JEHL ee koh). A delicious liqueur made with wild hazelnuts.
- *Grappa* (GRAW pah). The "high-octane" (50 to 60 percent alcohol) product distilled from pomace, the grape skin and pit leftovers that result from the wine-making process. Originally produced only in the colder northeastern regions of Trentino–Alto Adige, Friuli, and Veneto, grappa served to stave off the chill of winter and soothe the battered soul. Today the fame of grappa has spread throughout Italy and beyond, and this rough, raw product has become a highly favored, sophisticated option for ending a meal throughout the country. Great attention has been paid to refining the grappa-making process and to the packaging and marketing of the newly improved product in beautiful glass bottles. Quality grappa is produced today in several regions in the north, including Emilia-Romagna, Friuli–Venezia Giulia, Piemonte, Toscana, Trentino–Alto Adige, and Umbria. (See Market Buying Tips: *Grappa*.)
- *Mirto* (MEER toh). An alcoholic after-dinner liqueur made from myrtle. It's a product of Sardegna. (See Regional/Seasonal Specialties: Sardegna: *Mirto*.)
- *Sambuca* (sahm BOO kah). The delightful anise-

flavored liqueur served *con le mosche*, with three coffee beans nicknamed "flies," floating on top. The liqueur is made using the berries of the elder shrub.

Est! Est! Est! (AYST!). Literally, "It Is!" three times. It's the name of a famous white wine, Vernaccia, from Lazio. Legend has it that in the year 1110, a wine-loving German cardinal was about to travel to Rome for the coronation of Holy Roman Emperor Henry V. Concerned about the availability of good wines, he sent a messenger ahead to scout out the possibilities, telling him to post the word *"Est!"* on the door. When the cardinal arrived in the town of Montefiascone, he discovered his drunken messenger at a tavern upon whose door was written the enthusiastic message *"Est! Est! Est!"*

Gassosa (gahs SO sah). Carbonated drinks or soda.

Latte (LAT tay). Milk.

Limonata (lee moh NAH tah). A nonalcoholic lemon-flavored drink.

Marsala (mahr SAH lah). A fortified wine, produced in Sicily. (See Menu Primer A to Z: *Zabaione*, Comfort Foods: Veal, Regional/Seasonal Specialties: Lombardia: Introduction and *Piccata al marsala*, Sicilia: Introduction, and Market Buying Tips: *Marsala*.)

Seltz (SELTZ). Soda water.

Spremuta (spreh MOO tah). Freshly squeezed citrus juice. When it's billed as *di arancia* (ah RAN chah), it's freshly squeezed orange juice. *Di pompelmo* (pom PEHL moh) indicates freshly squeezed grapefruit juice.

Thè or *Tè* (TEH). Tea. To ask for tea with milk, request it *al latte* (LAT tay). When it's served with a lemon slice, it's *al limone* (lee MOH neh).

Tisana (tee SAH nah). This is the general name for herbal tea.

Vin santo (VEEN SAHN toh). This is a velvet-textured dessert wine produced predominantly in Toscana and Umbria, although there is some made in Trentino as well. You'll find it served most often with dry cookies like Toscana's *biscottini di Prato*. Quality varies widely, as does the degree of sweetness. The wine is made from late-harvest white grapes that are air-dried before being pressed and sealed in barrels for at least three years. Although *vin santo* translates as "holy wine," it does not suggest a role in religious services. According to legend, the name reflects the considerable enthusiasm a certain Cardinale Bessarione felt for the wine when he was introduced to it following a banquet. (See Menu Primer A to Z: *Biscotti* and *Cantucci* and Regional/Seasonal Specialties: Toscana: *Biscottini di Prato*.)

Vino (VEE noh). Wine. Who can imagine the food of Italy without wine? Traditionally very "approachable," or well-liked by the general public, Italian wines are meant to be drunk with food, and the quality in recent years has far surpassed the stereotypic *Chianti* (kee AHN tee) in the straw-covered bottle. The romance of Italian food and wine dates back at least as far as the arrival of the ancient Greeks, who astutely called the southern portion of the peninsula Enotria, or "Land of Wine." Today the soil remains hospitable, vineyards dot the landscape throughout the peninsula, and wine production remains a major force in the economy.

Italy's diverse geography, climate, and customs have created countless variations in grape preferences and wine-making techniques. Many of the regional wines are produced in such small quantities that they never make it to international markets. That's why it's such a joy to discover a local wine in a small town or village, often the house wine, *vino della casa* (VEE noh deh lah KAH sah), which many times is the ideal accompaniment to the local *cucina* (koo CHEE nah). These wines are often served not from bottles but in carafes of varying sizes. Beware, however, that in the larger cities, the house wine may be less than wonderful.

The changes in wine-making techniques and the increasingly sophisticated knowledge of many wine makers have altered the face of wine making in Italy. Now more and more attuned to worldwide market preferences, some Italian wine makers have replaced traditional grape varieties with better-known, more marketable ones, trading cultural heritage for profit. Most bottled wines are divided into two categories. One such label is DOC, for *"Denominazione di Origine Controllata."* DOC wines are controlled by laws that strictly determine grape variety, character, yield, and aging requirements, as well as geographic origin. The other distinction is DOCG, in which the G stands for a guarantee, or *"Garantita,"* that the wine meets these DOC characteristics. In theory, these designations have led to better quality control. But many wine makers chafe at these "controls" and prefer to create wines according to the old traditions or to experiment with new concepts. These wines are sold under the name *vino da tavola* (VEE noh dah TAH vo lah), "table wine," and range from the sublime to, shall we say, the uninspired.

COMFORT FOODS

· ■ ·

No MATTER how sophisticated one may be, there are times when only the familiar tastes of home will do, especially after many days or weeks of experimenting with exotic fare. This section offers a few dishes you can find in Italy that may be at least reminiscent of the dishes you might be craving.

Beef—*Bue* (Boo ay)—or beefsteak—*Bistecca* (bees TEK kah). *Arrosto* (ah ROAS toh) suggests roast loin of beef, which is most often the prime rib. *Ferri* (FER ree) indicates that the steak has been grilled. *Stracotto* (strah KOT toh) might just hit the spot. It's a pot roast, for which beef is braised slowly for many hours, usually with tomatoes, perhaps other vegetables, and red wine.
Bread. *Pane* (PAH nay).
Chicken. *Pollo* (POL loh).

• *Arrosto* (ah ROAS toh). Roast chicken, a frequent item on the menu. It's often flavored simply with fresh herbs like rosemary or sage and garlic.

- *Cacciatora, alla* (kaht chah TOH rah). "Hunter's style," which will vary from region to region. In general, the chicken is browned in oil and cooked with vegetables such as onion, celery, herbs, and often tomatoes and mushrooms, then braised with wine.
- *Costoletta di* (kos toh LET tah). Indicates a chicken cutlet, often braised with a sauce of tomato (*pomodoro*—pom oh DAW roh) and mushrooms (*funghi*—FOON ghee).
- *Fritto* (FREET toh). The word to look for if it's fried chicken you're craving; it will probably be marinated first in olive oil, lemon juice, and fresh herbs, then breaded and fried.
- *Milanese, alla* (meel ahn AY zay). Milan-style. It's floured, dipped in egg, breaded, and then pan-fried.
- *Petto di pollo* (PEYT toh). Breast of chicken. There are an infinite number of preparations. Here's a sampling of the more familiar:
  —*Petto di pollo alla bolognese* (boh loh NYAY zay). Bologna-style; it will be floured, egg-dipped, and fried in butter, then covered with a slice of prosciutto and cheese and briefly run under the broiler.
  —*Petto di pollo al limone* (lee MOH neh) or *alla Lombardia* (lohm BAHR dya). Chicken flavored with lemon and parsley.

(See Menu Primer A to Z: *Pollo.*)

Coffee. *Caffè.* (kah FAY). (See Beverages A to Z: *Caffè.*)

Eggplant Parmesan. *Parmigiana di melanzane* (pahr

mee GYAH nah dee mey lahn TSAH ney). The southern regions of Italy spawned this worldwide favorite, which still appears here in both pizza parlors and more upscale restaurants, especially in the southern regions. It will probably resemble the dish served back home, except that the tomato sauce may be lighter than the *ragù* that often adorns the dish in America and the mozzarella might have more flavor! The eggplant will be sliced, floured, and fried in olive oil, then layered in a baking dish with the tomato sauce and slices of mozzarella and perhaps a few basil leaves. It is then topped with Parmesan and baked.

Fish. *Pesce* (PAY shay). Fish is generally prepared very simply in Italy so as not to mask its freshness and true flavor. But many of the selections will be unfamiliar to you, and the names can change from region to region. A simple preparation for fish that's found all over the country is listed either as *ai ferri* (ay FER ree) (literally, "on iron") or *alla griglia* (ah lah GREEL yah), meaning that the fish has been grilled on a ridged or flat pan or grill after marinating in olive oil and herbs. Fried (often deep-fried) fish or seafood will be described as *fritto* (FREET toh). (See Menu Primer A to Z: *Pesce.*)

Fruit. *Frutta* (FROOT tah). You'll find wonderfully fresh, seasonal fruits at the markets and on menus. Apples, *mela* (MEY lah), from Trentino–Alto Adige are exceptional. Peaches, *pesche* (PES kay), are a springtime treat, especially the white peaches grown in the lagoon of Venezia. Tiny wild strawberries, called *fragoline* (frah goh LEE nay), also herald springtime. Melons are called *melone* (mey LOH nay); you'll most often see cantaloupe *(cantaloup)*. In the southern regions, excellent oranges, *arancia* (ah RAN chah), are produced, including the *tarocco* (tah ROK koh), the aptly named "blood orange" with its bright red flesh! (They taste just like the orange-colored ones.) And you'll find wonderful grapes, *uva* (OO vah), both green and purple, in late summer and fall.

Meatballs. *Polpette* (pohl PET teh). In Italy, meatballs are not served atop your spaghetti. If they're cooked with a sauce, the sauce is served over pasta and the meatballs follow as the next course. Meatballs are traditionally made with beef or lamb, milk-soaked bread, garlic, Parmesan, and spices and cooked in a tomato sauce. *Polpette alla napoletana* (nah poh lay TAH nah) are made with ground beef, grated Parmesan, garlic, and herbs, then cooked in a tomato sauce. This version is probably most like "home" because much of the traditional Italian food here in America is southern Italian cooking, as it was mostly southern Italians who emigrated to America in the early part of the century. (See Menu Primer A to Z: *Polpette*.)

Pasta. *Pasta* (PAH stah). This is the prime starch consumed in Italy, whether it's handmade egg pasta or the commercial dried pasta from a factory. These are a few of the more familiar preparations:

• Fettuccine Alfredo. *Fettuccine Alfredo* (fet too CHEE nee ahl FRAY doh) is the rich and creamy favorite known worldwide. The sauce, named for the

Roman restaurateur who made both the sauce and himself rich and famous, contains butter, *parmigiano-reggiano* (pahr mee GYA noh reh JAHN oh), and sometimes, but not always, cream. In Italy, it's usually served over homemade egg pasta fettuccine.

- Lasagna. *Lasagne* (lah ZHAN yay) is usually made in Italy with fresh, not dried, pasta and layered with a variety of fillings. The bolognese version is made with meat sauce (*ragù*), béchamel, and *parmigiano-reggiano*. The hearty southern *lasagne* boast sausage, meat sauce, or even meatballs, in tomato sauce, and mozzarella. Other versions may be layered with artichokes or *ricotta* (ree KOHT tah) mixed with *pesto* (PEY stoh.)

- Linguine with clam sauce. *Linguine alla vongole* (leen GWEE nay ah lah VON goh lay). This dish is especially good made with the clams from the Adriatic, which are small and full of flavor. The sauce may be red, *rosso* (ROS soh), or white, *bianco* (bee AHN koh). Garlic is a given!

- Macaroni. *Maccheroni* (mahk keh ROH nee). The term encompasses all tubular pastas, from *penne* (PEYN nay) (quill- or pen-shaped) to *rigatoni* (ree gah TOH nee) (broad, short tubes) to *ziti* (TSEE tee) (narrow, short tubes). The tiny macaroni we know is called *maccheroncini*, and it may be paired with a creamy sauce, along with vegetables, ham, or perhaps some gorgonzola. (No Velveeta here!)

- *Marinara, alla* (mah ree NAH rah). "Sailor's style" sauce, which usually resembles the tomato-based red sauce so familiar in Italian-American restaurants back home, but in Italy it can also contain black olives and capers.

- *Pasta al pomodoro* (pom oh DAW roh). A simple olive oil–based tomato sauce cooked with onion, garlic, and herbs.
- *Spaghetti e polpette* (pohl PET teh). Many people are surprised to find that spaghetti and meatballs are not served together in Italy. (See Comfort Foods: Meatballs.)

Pizza. *Pizza* (PEET tsah). Ready-made slices of pizza displayed in the windows of fast-food shops are *not* your best bet. Pizza is best when cooked to order in a real pizzeria that boasts a wood-burning brick oven. Toppings range from the minimalist *napoletana* (nah pohl eh TAHN ah) topped with just tomatoes, garlic, and oregano, to the *capricciosa* (kah pree CHOH sah), the "capricious" one, topped, as one might imagine, at the whim, or the supply list, of the pizza chef, or *pizzaiolo* (peet tsay YOH loh), with everything from mushrooms and olives to slices of hot dog!

- *Calzone* (kahl TSOH nay). In this dish, the dough is filled, usually with cheese, ham, and salami, then folded over into a half-moon and topped with tomato sauce, much like a turnover.
- *Focaccia* (foh KAH chyah), *Schiacciata* (skyaht CHYAH tah), or *Piadina* (pyah DEE nah). These are some of the flatbreads, and both the names

and the toppings vary from region to region. The bread can be soft or crisp, puffy or thin, flavored with an unending array of toppings, some as simple as fresh herbs, salt, and olive oil, others with local cheeses, garlic, or anchovies. Sweet focacci are found as well, as in the delightful Bolognese version that serves as an envelope for a dynamite ice-cream sandwich! (See Menu Primer A to Z: *Focaccia, Piadina,* and *Schiacciata* and Regional/Seasonal Specialties: Basilicata: *Focaccia al miele,* Campania: *Pizza,* and Emilia-Romagna: *Piadina.*)

- *Margherita* (mahr gey REE tah). It has traveled to America pretty well intact—it has tomatoes, mozzarella, olive oil, and fresh basil leaves—the three colors of the Italian flag.
- *Marinara* (mahr ee NAH rah). Made with tomatoes, garlic, and anchovies.
- *Napoletana.* From the birthplace of pizza, Napoli. It's the classic, with tomatoes, garlic, and oregano.
- *Quattro stagioni* (KWAHT roh stah JOH nee). Literally translated as "four seasons." Instead of mixing all topping ingredients together, this pizza is divided into four parts, each quadrant topped separately, one with mushrooms—*funghi* (FOON ghee), the others with olives—*olive* (oh LEE vey), artichoke hearts—*carciofi* (kahr CHOH fee), and *prosciutto* (pro SHOOT toh). It's ideal for the purists in the party!

- *Romana.* Can be topped with tomatoes (or sometimes not!), but it should include mozzarella, basil, and anchovies.
- *Rustica* (ROOS tee kah). Another version of the stuffed dough concept; it's made in the form of a tart, with a top and a bottom crust. The filling can include cheeses such as pecorino, mozzarella, provolone, and ricotta along with ham, onion, peppers, and/or spinach.

Other single topping ingredients include:

- *Cipolla* (chee POL lah). Onion.
- *Frutti di mare* (FROOT tee dee MAH ray). Seafood.
- *Prosciutto* (pro SHOOT toh). Ham.
- *Salsiccia* (sahl SEET chyah). Sausage.
- *Vongole* (VON goh lay). Clams.
- *Wurstel* (VOOR stehl). Hot dog slices.

Pork. *Maiale* (mah YAH lay). Pork is available throughout Italy, both fresh or cured in the form of *salumi*, a means of preserving it. *Arista* (ah REES tah) is a term you will see frequently. It indicates roast saddle or loin of pork that's been oven- or spit-roasted. In Toscana, the fresh roasted pork is most often flavored with a paste of garlic, cloves, and rosemary. Another favorite is flavored with sage leaves—*alla salvia* (SAHL vyah). *Carre di maiale* (KAHR reh) also refers to a roasted loin or saddle of pork. *Costolette* (or *cotolette*) *di maiale* (kos toh LET tay or kot oh LET tay) are pork chops or cutlets. *Lombo*, or *lombata*, (LOHM boh or lohm BAHT tah) are fried or sautéed slices of pork loin that may be sauced in any number of ways. (See Menu Primer A to Z: *Maiale*.)

Sandwich. *Panino* (pah NEE noh) or *Tramezzino* (trah met TSEE noh). The sandwich bar *(paninoteca)* abounds, with either ready-made or made-to-order offerings. These sandwiches are usually filled with some sort of ham or *salumi*. Cheese on a roll, sometimes "pressed" and grilled, is also offered. To order a slightly more familiar grilled ham and cheese on American-style bread, ask for a *toast* (TOST)! Most American sandwiches such as tuna or chicken salad are not to be found, but other items you'll find tucked between two slices of bread or a roll include vegetable frittata (omelette) and breaded veal cutlet topped with cheese!

Seafood. *Frutti di mare* (FROOT tee dee MAH ray). *Scampi* is the Italian word for "shrimp," which may also be referred to as *gamberi* (gam BEH ree) or *gamberetti* (gahm bey RET tee), which are the small shrimp or prawns. *Gamberi* are regular-sized prawns, and *gamberoni* (gam behr OH nee) refers to the large size. They are often prepared boiled—*bollito* (bol LEE toh)—or fried—*fritto* (FREET toh). Clams, called *vongole* (VOHN goh lay), are a familiar partner with pasta. Delicious scallops, *cape sante* (KAH pay SAHN tay), are often available in the coastal regions, as are mussels, *cozze* (KOH tsay).

They are both prepared simply, perhaps steamed or braised. (See Menu Primer A to Z: *Cape sante, Cozze, Gamberetti,* and *Vongole*.)

Soup. *Minestra* (mee NES trah) or *Zuppa* (TSOOP pah). Broth in Italy can be made from chicken, *di pollo* (POL loh), or beef, *di manzo* (MAHN zoh). The broth is often served with some type of pasta. Cream soups will be marked *di crema* (KREH mah), and could be tomato, *di pomodoro* (pom oh DAW roh), mushroom, *di funghi* (FOON ghee), or other vegetables, according to the season. The ever-popular *minestrone* (mee nes TROH nay) will vary according to the region and season but will always contain vegetables, thickened with rice, beans, or pasta. (See Menu Primer A to Z: All listings under *Minestra* and Regional/Seasonal Specialties: Abruzzo: *Zuppa di scarola virtu*, Basilicata: *Grano e ceci*, Friuli–Venezia Giulia: *Minestra d'orzo e fagioli, Minestra con i finocchi,* Toscana: *Pappa col pomodoro, Pasta e fagioli,* and *Ribollita*, Trentino–Alto Adige: *Minestra d'orzo,* and Umbria: *Minestra di farro*.)

Veal. *Vitello* (vee TEHL loh) is served often in Italy. Veal dishes are typically named just by the cut of meat such as *scaloppini* instead of the full *scaloppine di vitello* or veal scallop. *Costolette di vitello* (kos toh LET tay) is a veal cutlet. If the dish is *arrosto* (ah ROAS toh), or *al forno* (FOR noh), it's simply a roast, usually the loin or leg. From Milano comes the famous veal marsala (mahr SAH lah), flavored with the popular fortified wine. The familiar veal Parmesan, usually called *scaloppine alla parmigiana* on the

Italian menu, can be dipped in egg, then rolled in a combination of Parmesan and bread crumbs, then fried in butter or, breaded and fried, topped with a slice of Parmesan (or fontina) and run under the broiler. Veal *piccata* (peek KAH tah) consists of thin cutlets, cooked in butter and lemon. (See Menu Primer A to Z: *Vitello.*)

REGIONAL/SEASONAL
SPECIALTIES

· ■ ·

Because the land known to us as Italy is, in historical terms, a relatively new entity (it became a unified nation in 1870), distinct regional differences remain remarkably intact, even today. This fact allows us to experience wide variations in culture and tastes within its boundaries. This section will give a thumbnail sketch of each region and feature the "not-to-be-missed" specialties that may not be found outside its borders.

ABRUZZO AND THE MOLISE

Mountains cover two thirds of the regions of Abruzzo and the Molise, and a significant percentage of the remaining land is hilly, leaving just a small strip of flatland on the coast by the Adriatic Sea. Up until 1963, the two regions were one, but in that year, the Molise became independent of its neighbor to the north. Although the basic ingredients available to the two regions were essentially the same, the *cucina* of Molise was molded by an unusual cultural phenomenon. Traditionally, the Molisani were shepherds, and each winter they would find it necessary to migrate from the mountains down to the lowlands in search of grazing land for their sheep and cattle. This constant movement, called *transumanza*, created the necessity for foods that were made quickly and easily transported. Vegetables such as cardoons and broccoli rabe, wild greens, simple pastas, bread, olive oil, and wine were the standard fare, and dinner was a one-dish affair rather than a drawn-out meal consisting of many courses.

For centuries, the Abruzzesi and Molisani were cut off from their neighbors and forced to eke out a meager existence, raising sheep and pigs, farming, or fishing. Cooks were forced to focus all their skills on very limited (although excellent) resources. This concentration of effort has resulted in the creation of a few superb specialties.

Lamb dishes are found here as are cheeses made from sheep's milk. The frugal Abruzzesi and Molisani waste nothing; there is even a dish made from the remains in the pantry at the end of the winter—some chickpeas, perhaps, or a few lentils, any leftover vegetables, and the bone from the prosciutto. Some of the finest pasta has been produced here, including the most celebrated of this region, *maccheroni alla chitarra*. Abruzzo exports a good deal of its excellent pasta. (See Market Buying Tips: *Pasta*.) And although imported spices were virtually unknown, hot red chili peppers grew readily and are found in almost all savory dishes. Of note as well is the saffron, *zafferano*, some of the world's finest. Fish and seafood are drawn from the Adriatic, and the renowned fish stew, *brodetto,* usually made spicy with the addition of red chili peppers, is one of the best in all of Italy.

Over the past thirty years, improved methods of communication and transportation have paved the way for increased contact, but, although adjacent to Lazio, Abruzzo and the Molise have not attracted huge numbers of tourists, except for those drawn to the mountains to ski. The resulting paucity of restaurants can make it difficult to sample the specialties. If you're lucky enough to be "in the neighborhood" at just the right time, you might want to partake in the celebration called *panarda,* an exuberant ritual feast day, or *sagre,* of the region that seems to belie the very nature of these frugal people. Many of the festivals all over Italy celebrate the harvest, or, as in this case, the killing of the pig. No other region celebrates this ritual as lavishly. In Abruzzo, *panarda* is a virtual marathon of a meal consisting of at least thirty courses and large quantities of homemade wine, an astonishing exception to the culture's usual moderation!

Agnello alla griglia. Grilled lamb. (See Menu Primer A to Z: *Agnello.*)

Agnello all'uovo e limone (an YEL loh ahl oo WO voh ay lee MOH nay). A delicious regional lamb dish with egg and lemon that celebrates springtime and is served traditionally at Easter.

Brodetto di pesce (broh DET toh dee PAY shay). In Abruzzo, this is a highly regarded fish soup, usually made *very* spicy with the ubiquitous chili peppers, *peperoncini* (pey pey rohn CHEE nee), as well as garlic, olive oil, and either sweet red pepper or tomato.

Cassata abruzzese (kah SAH tah ah broo TZAY zay). This is the *abruzzese* version of the southern Italian favorite, sponge cake layered with rich custard and flavored with bits of chocolate and caramel.

Formaggio di pecora (for MAHD joh dee PEK oh rah), or *marcetto* (mar CHET toh). The sheep's cheese of the region is sharp in flavor and soft in texture.

Insalata di frutti di mare. Seafood salad. (See Menu Primer A to Z: *Insalata di mare.*)

Mortadella (mor tah DEHL lah). This is the large, smooth *salume* made with pork liver and pistachio nuts, but in this region it's flavored with orange peel and citron

Pasta

- *Calcioni di ricotta* (kahl CHOH nee dee ree KOHT tah). These are a specialty of the town of Campobasso in the Molise. These stuffed pastas are fried and served alongside a mixture of deep-fried vegetables, organ meats, and the region's famous cheese, scamorza.
- *Gnocchi* (NYOH kee). Delicious potato and flour

dumplings are especially good here in Abruzzo because they're made with the flavorful local potatoes.

- *Maccheroni alla chitarra* (mahk keh ROH nee ah lah kee TAHR rah). It's pasta "guitar-style." Created in the 1700s, this square-shaped spaghetti is made by cutting large sheets of fresh egg pasta into strips with a device that resembles a guitar, consisting of steel wires stretched on a wooden frame. The pasta is usually served with a tomato-based sauce, often made spicy with chilies and flavored with some pork product, perhaps pancetta or *guanciale* (hog's jowl), and topped with pecorino (sheep's cheese).
- *Ravioli all'Abruzzo* (rah VYOH lee ahl ah BRUTS soh). These are cheese-filled pasta squares made either savory or sweet. The savory ones are filled with the local cheese scamorza, the sweet ones with *ricotta* (ree KOHT tah).
- *Scrippelle* (skree PEHL lay). The local word for crepes—they're called *crespelle* (kres PEHL lay) in other parts of Italy. They're served either in broth, sauced, or baked with cheese.

Patate alle olive (pah TAH teh ahl lay oh LEE veh). Potatoes are cooked with olive oil, capers, anchovies, and parsley. Simple dishes with strong flavors are found throughout Abruzzo and the Molise.

Salsiccie di fegato (sal SEET chay dee feh GAH toh). Sausage made from pork liver. Some, called *fegato pazzo* (feh GAH toh PAHT tsoh), literally "crazy liver," are made hot with the *peperoncini* (pey pey rohn CHEE nee) or chili peppers. The *fegato dolce* (feh GAH toh DOL chay), sweetened with honey, is milder. The two types are meant to be eaten together, alternating the hot with the sweet!

Scamorza (skah MOR tzah). A firm-textured, buttery-tasting sheep's cheese. (See Menu Primer A to Z: *Scamorza*.)

Trippa in umido (TREEP pah een OO mee doh). Tripe, which in Abruzzo is from sheep, is boiled until tender, then stewed with onion, carrot, celery, tomatoes, and often fennel seeds and topped with grated sheep's cheese—pecorino—and parsley. (See Menu Primer A to Z: *Trippa*.)

Virtù (veer TOO). A rich soup, traditionally containing forty-nine ingredients, including vegetables, meat, pastas, and beans.

Zuppa di scarola (TSOOP pah dee skah ROH lah). Escarole, or curly endive, soup. First-class vegetables such as escarole are grown in Abruzzo and used to make delicious soups, flavored with onions, garlic, a little pork fat and topped with grated pecorino (sheep's cheese).

BASILICATA

Situated in the instep of the boot of Italy, Basilicata is rather an oddity in that densely inhabited country, a sparsely populated region where only two towns, Potenza and Matera, have more than fifty thousand residents. The mountainous terrain, coupled with small "windows" on the sea, have shaped the *cucina* of Basilicata. Traditionally, wild hare and fowl were hunted and sheep and pigs were raised, but meat was a rarity in the diet of these impoverished people. Fish and seafood were available only on the two tiny coasts, but that connection with the sea gave conquerors from the Near East access to Basilicata. Greek and Byzantine influences are still apparent in the many dishes containing almonds, cinnamon, and cloves. Legumes, including fava beans, chickpeas, and lentils, appear in soups, salads, and vegetable dishes.

Today, increased affluence has increased the availability of animal protein in the diet. The irony, of course, is that *la cucina povera,* or "cooking of the poor," including vegetables, fruits, legumes, pasta, and olive oil, provide a diet that nutritionists today tout as the healthiest.

Agnello al forno (ahn YEL loh ahl FOR noh). In Basilicata, lamb is often oven-roasted with olive oil and lard and flavored with wild herbs, especially oregano.

Agnello con funghi (FOON ghee). This is a delicious combination of lamb and the region's fresh mushrooms called *cardoncelli* (kahr dohn CHEL lee), spiced with hot red pepper. The dish can be stewed or sautéed.

Bignè al cioccolato (been NYAY ahl choh koh LAH toh). These are pastries filled with dark chocolate.

Burrata (boo RAH tah). Delicious soft cheese of the region, made from cow's milk.

Ciamotta (chyah MOT tah). This is a mixed vegetable stew in which the individual vegetables are fried separately, then combined. It's made with eggplant, tomatoes, peppers, and sometimes potatoes and it's flavored with garlic. With the emphasis on vegetables and legumes in the region of Basilicata, the vegetable course is often the main event!

Ciaudedda (chyahoo DAYD dah). Fava beans are cooked in olive oil with potatoes, onions, and artichokes.

Focaccia al miele (foh KAH chyah ahl mee AY lay). This is a sweet flatbread topped with honey.

Grano e ceci (GRAH noh ay CHEH chee). Soup made with some type of grain such as barley and wheat along with chickpeas and tomato and flavored with herbs.

Lucanica (loo kah NEE kah). The marvelous spiced sausage of Basilicata, usually served grilled as an antipasto, but it's also used to spice up pasta dishes.

Maiale all'alloro (mah YAH lay ahl ahl LOH roh). Pork is browned in olive oil, then flavored with bay leaves, juniper berries, cloves, onion, and white wine.

Mandorlata di peperoni (mahn dor LAH tah dee pey pey ROH nee). This is a regional vegetable stew, made with almonds, sweet peppers, and fiery-hot *peperoncini*.

Pasta

- *Lagane con lenticchie e fagioli* (lah GHAN eh kon len TEE kee ay fah JOH lee). This dish is made with lasagnalike noodles, but it's not baked. Instead, the noodles are cooked and tossed with lentils and beans and sometimes tomato.
- *Maccheroni di fuoco* (mahk keh ROH nee dee FWAW koh). Thick strands of spaghetti called bucatini are cooked with the fiery sauce named *diavolicchio* (dee ah voh LEE kyoh). The dish is not for the faint of heart!
- *Orecchiette al pomodoro* (oh rek KYET teh ahl pom oh DAW roh). Large ear-shaped pasta, sometimes called *scorze di mandorla* (SKOR tseh dee mahn DOR lah), or almond skins, is sauced with tomato and topped with pecorino (sheep's cheese).
- *Pastizz* (pahs TEETS). This is another name for calzone (kal TSOH nay), a pasta turnover usually filled with lamb or pork but sometimes with vegetables.

Provola (PRO voh lah). This is a cheese traditionally made from buffalo milk, usually smoked to improve its keeping qualities. These days, it's more likely to be made with cow's milk.

Zuppa di pesce (TSOOP pah dee PAY shay). The local fish soup or stew is made hot and spicy with the addition of the fiery sauce *diavolicchio* (dee ah voh LEE kyoh). The sauce, made with the hot, usually red, peppers of the region called *peperoncini*, spices up many of the dishes of Basilicata.

CALABRIA

Like much of southern Italy, Calabria, situated in the toe of the Italian boot, is a mix of harsh mountainous terrain and seacoast. Throughout history, the inhabitants of this impoverished region were constantly besieged by conquering forces. Consequently, the Calabrians became a closed and patriarchal people, suspicious of outsiders, with loyalty to the family, and the accompanying interfamily feuding, becoming a way of life. Much of the emigration from Italy to America around the beginning of the twentieth century was from the south, and the dishes that we think of as Italian, including eggplant Parmesan, were part of the Calabrian repertoire.

The cuisine reflects the poverty of the south, which is not to say that quality is absent. It is based on the available fruits of the land and the sea, and what delicious fruits they are! Olives, grapes, fish, snails, game, vegetables, almonds, and figs are the basis of the *cucina*, and the reserved and insular nature of the people has resulted in few changes over the centuries.

The vegetable course in Calabria often serves as the main course, or *secondo*. Eggplant appears on the table in countless preparations. It's stuffed, fried, stewed, layered with cheese and baked, and cooked *all'agro-dolce*—sweet and sour—a leftover influence of the Eastern invaders. Tomatoes, sweet and hot peppers, artichokes, mushrooms, cabbage, and onions are staples as is pasta. Brides traditionally came to the altar with the ability to make several different shapes of home-made pasta. Delicious tuna and swordfish play a large role in the diet of the coastal inhabitants, while sheep and goats (and their cheeses), as well as pigs and wild game, provide the animal protein in the mountains. Fresh or dried fruits and nuts often end a meal in Calabria. Most pastries are reserved for feast days. Citrus fruits (especially citron, whose pebbly skin is candied and used in desserts throughout Italy) and bergamot (what you smell and taste when you drink Earl Grey tea) abound here, along with superb figs and almonds.

Caciocavallo (kah chyoh kah VAHL loh) or *caciu* (kah CHOO). This is a cheese commonly found in the southern parts of the peninsula. Aging the cheese changes the taste from mild to sharp. (See Menu Primer A to Z: *Caciu*.)

Capocollo (kah poh KOHL loh). A cured pork *salumi* made mostly in the southern regions. (See Menu Primer A to Z: *Capocollo*.)

Ceci all'olio (CHEH chee ahl OL yoh). This simple antipasto of chickpeas in olive oil is flavored with garlic and onion, salt, and lots of black pepper. It's served most often at Christmas.

Cinghiale allo spiedo (cheen GYAH ley ah loh SPYEY doh). From the mountain tradition comes the hunting of wild boar, which in this case is seasoned with herbs such as rosemary and fennel, skewered, and roasted over a charcoal fire.

Fichi ripieni (FEE kee ree PYAY nee). The delicious figs of Calabria are dried, then stuffed with a filling, such as almonds, chocolate, or candied fruits. *Fichi mandorlati* (mahn dor LAH tee) have almond stuffing.

Mariola (mahr YOH lah). Leftover cooked frittata, or omelette, sliced and served in a broth (usually chicken). This is an excellent example of how the poor made the most of every morsel of food.

Melanzane alla scapece (mey lahn TSAH nay ah lah skah PAY chay). This popular southern Italian appetizer is made from slices of eggplant pickled in white wine vinegar, olive oil, garlic, red pepper flakes, and oregano. It is delicious as an antipasto or on a slice of crusty bread.

Millecosedde (MEEL leh koh SED deh). Literally, this is the soup of a "thousand little things"—beans, legumes, cabbage, mushrooms, onions, carrots, pasta—whatever is available, cooked in chicken broth and topped with grated cheese.

Parmigiana di melanzane (pahr mee GYAH nah dee mey lahn TSAH ney). The famous eggplant Parmesan served throughout the southern regions of Italy. It's comprised of slices of meaty eggplant that are breaded and fried, then baked with tomato sauce, mozzarella, and *parmigiano-reggiano*.

Pasta

- *Bucatini* (or *Perciatelle*) *ammundicata* (boo kah TEE nee or per chah TEHL lay ahm moon dee KAH tah). These thick, hollow strands of spaghetti are cooked with olive oil, red pepper flakes, and anchovies, then topped with toasted bread crumbs. This humble dish is packed with flavor.
- *Maccheroni alla pastora.* This is pasta "shepherd's style." It consists of small lengths of hollow pasta, usually penne, rigatoni, ziti, or bucatini, that have been broken into short pieces and topped with pork sausage, ricotta (ree KOHT tah), red and black pepper, and grated sheep's cheese.
- *Rigatoni saltati* (ree gah TOH nee sahl TAH tee). A hearty, rustic pasta, once served only on special occasions because it contains a generous amount of meat, often a combination of pork, lamb, and turkey, simmered with red wine and onions. It's served with the ridged *maccheroni* called rigatoni, and topped with grated cheese.

Pesce spada (PAY shay SPAH dah). Swordfish. (See Menu Primer A to Z: *Pesce spada.*)

Porcini (por CHEE nee). In the mountainous territory of Calabria, these mushrooms grow wild and are celebrated with a *sagre,* or festival, in the fall. (See Menu Primer A to Z: *Porcini* and Market Buying Tips: *Funghi.*)

Provolone (pro voh LOH neh). A popular regional cheese that has also become well known in the rest of the world, provolone is usually found aged and somewhat sharp.

Salsiccia (sahl SEET chah). Sausage made from pork is a common protein source in the region. (See Menu Primer A to Z: *Salsiccia.*)

Soppressata (soh preh SAH tah). Blood sausage. (See Menu Primer A to Z: *Soppressata.*)

Tonno alla calabrese (TOHN noh ah lah kahl ah BRAY zay). Freshly caught tuna, generally baked with olive oil, bread crumbs, red pepper flakes, and marinara sauce. There are countless other preparations of tuna, especially in the town of Pizzo. (See Menu Primer A to Z: *Tonno.*)

Zeppole (ZEP poh leh). These delicious fried cream puffs are available especially at Christmas.

CAMPANIA

The happy convergence of fertile volcanic soil, idyllic climate, and seacoast has provided Campania with the ingredients for a *cucina* based on exquisite vegetables and fruits, grazing land for cattle (and their by-product, cheese), hard durum wheat for pasta, and excellent seafood. The locals tend to attack life—and their dinner—with gusto. The food of Campania—pizza, eggplant Parmesan, lasagna, and spaghetti with tomato sauce—are what most Americans have traditionally thought of as "Italian food." Since most of the Italian immigrants around the turn of the century came from the impoverished southern regions, theirs was the style of cooking first introduced to America.

Pizza has conquered the culinary world, but it was born in Naples, where all the elements—the water, the tomatoes from the vines, the oil from the olives, the fragrant basil, the flavorful mozzarella, and the skilled hands of the *pizzaioli*, or pizza makers—conspire to create what aficionados know as *the definitive pizza!* And the combination of hard wheat for making first-class commercial pasta and the ideal climate for drying the pasta has created a very serious pasta tradition in Campania.

The mozzarella made in this region is as good as it gets. The most highly prized is that made from the milk of water buffalo, *mozzarella di bufala*, but it's relatively scarce, and cheese made with cow's milk, *fior di latte,* is more common. The *bufala mozzarella* is thought by some Neapolitans to be too moist for making pizza (or too expensive), so the *fior di latte* is what you'll most likely find there.

Fish and seafood also play a large role in the cuisine. Swordfish, bass, *scampi* (shrimp), langoustines, squid, octopus, and countless others are drawn from the Mare Tirreno and are found on the antipasto menu, in *zuppa* (soup), or as the main course.

Braciole (bra CHYO lay). These are slices of steak, pounded thin, usually stuffed with prosciutto, provolone, and varying other ingredients, rolled tightly and cooked with tomatoes. The steak can also be left flat, topped with tomatoes, garlic, oregano, and oil just like a pizza and called—for obvious reasons—*alla pizzaiola*.

Fritto misto di pesce (FREET toh MEES toh dee PAY shay). This popular dish is usually made with a variety of fresh seafood—often *scampi*, langoustines, or baby squid—breaded, deep-fried, and served simply with lemon to squeeze on top and a dusting of parsley.

Insalata caprese (een sah LAH tah kah PRAY zay). A salad from the isle of Capri, where it was made traditionally with slices of *mozzarella di bufala* (BOOF fahl lah), tomato, and fresh basil leaves and anointed with olive oil. Today, cow's milk mozzarella is more common. (See Menu Primer A to Z: *Insalata caprese*.)

Insalata di mare (een sah LAH tah dee MAH ray). The plentiful seafood from the coastal waters often is served as this cold salad, dressed with lemon juice or vinegar and olive oil. (See Menu Primer A to Z: *Insalata di mare.*)

Melanzane alla mozzarella (mey lahn TSAH ney ah lah mot tzah REHL lah). Grilled slices of eggplant are topped with mozzarella, slices of fresh tomato, and basil.

Mozzarella in carozza (motz tzah REHL lah een kahr OTS sah). Deep-fried mozzarella, originally made with buffalo mozzarella (made from the milk of water buffalo), is now usually made with cow's milk, or *fior di latte.* Crusty bread encloses the cheese slice (and sometimes a slice of anchovy) and the whole thing is dipped in beaten egg, then deep-fried.

Parmigiana di melanzane (pahr mee GYAH nah dee mey lahn TSAN ney). This is the definitive eggplant Parmesan, probably the best known of the dishes to come from Campania, although it's found throughout southern Italy and its neighboring Mediterranean countries as well. Slices of eggplant are fried in olive oil and layered with a light, garlic-spiked tomato sauce and slices of mozzarella (not *parmigiano,* as one would assume). The dish is topped with *parmigiano* and some fresh basil leaves, then baked. (See Comfort Foods: Eggplant Parmesan.)

Pasta

- *Al forno* (FOR noh). This is a general term for baked pasta dishes, which are found throughout the region, using different pastas—lasagna, *maccheroni*, and ziti, for instance. They invariably contain tomato sauce and mozzarella and other cheeses, as well as vegetables such as eggplant or zucchini.

- *Alla sorrentina* (sohr rhen TEE nah). This is pasta in the style of Sorrento, with tomato and melted mozzarella.

- *Spaghetti aglio e olio* (AHL yoh ay OL yoh). One of the most modest of the sauces to grace the pasta of Campania, this topping of garlic and oil, and perhaps a little parsley and bread crumbs, is proof of the "less is more" philosophy. (See Menu Primer A to Z: *Pasta/Salse*.)

- *Spaghetti alla vongole*. This is the classic spaghetti with clam sauce, which can be white or red (with tomatoes). (See Menu Primer A to Z: *Pasta/Salse* and Comfort Foods: Pasta: Linguine with clam sauce, and Pizza.)

Pasta e fagioli (PAH stah ay fah JOH lee). This is hearty bean and pasta soup. (See Menu Primer A to Z: *Pasta e fagioli*.)

Pastiera (pahs TYAY rah). An outstanding classic cake from Naples, traditionally made for Easter, with *ricotta* (ree KOHT tah), lemon, raisins, and candied fruit.

Peperonata (pey pey roh NAH tah). The excellent sweet peppers of the region are cooked with tomatoes, olive oil, onion, garlic, and fresh oregano and basil to make a thick stew. *Peperonata* appears both as a side dish and as a pasta topping. (See Menu Primer A to Z: *Peperonata*.)

Pizza

- *Margherita* (mahr gey REE tah). Named for Margherita, the Queen of Savoy, this is probably the pizza you'll see most often, with tomatoes, mozzarella, and fresh basil leaves, representing the colors of the Italian flag. It's one dish that has traveled to America pretty well intact.
- *Marinara* (mahr ee NAH rah). Tomatoes and garlic top this one. There's no cheese, but sometimes you'll find anchovies.
- *Napoletana* (nah pohl eh TAHN ah). From Napoli comes the classic, with tomatoes, garlic, and oregano. (See Comfort Foods: Pizza.)

Pizzelle (pee TSEHL leh). "Little pizzas," often served as part of the meal, usually topped simply with tomato and Parmesan or ricotta (ree KOHT tah) and sautéed greens.

Polpo or *Polipo alla Luciana* (POL poh or poh LEE poh ah lah loo CHAH nah). Octopus is a specialty in Campania, where it is slow-cooked, usually in a ceramic casserole, with olive oil, garlic, parsley, and sometimes chili pepper or tomatoes. The tiny *polpo* are called *polpetielli* (pol pet YEL lee). (See Menu Primer A to Z: *Polpo*.)

Scapece (skah PAY chay). A method, typical of the southern regions, for preparing vegetables such as eggplant and zucchini or small fish such as sardines and anchovies by first frying them in olive oil, then marinating them in wine vinegar. Served often as an antipasto. (See Regional/Seasonal Specialties: Calabria: *Melanzane alla scapece*.)

Sfogliatelle (sfo lyah TEHL leh). These are delicious pastries, often served at breakfast filled with ricotta (ree KOHT tah) or pastry cream.

Spumone (spoo MOH ney). This is the frothy-textured ice cream, filled with fruit and nuts, that crossed the ocean with the immigrants.

EMILIA-ROMAGNA

The combined regions of Emilia and Romagna form a portion of Il Centro, the central part of Italy, and many of the foods for which Italy has become revered come from this rich heartland. Hailed by cognoscenti as the unrivaled leader in Italian gastronomy, the city of Bologna and Emilia-Romagna are nevertheless less well known to tourists. The fertile farmlands of Emilia yield wonderful fruits and vegetables and provide excellent grazing for livestock, producing superb meats and meat products as well as unsurpassed cheese, butter, and cream. Romagna, to the east, boasts not only the seafood bounty of its Adriatic coastline but also the grilled specialties of the Apennines.

The four cornerstones of gastronomic excellence in the region are *aceto balsamico*—balsamic vinegar; the cheese *parmigiano-reggiano*, arguably the finest cheese in Italy and, some would say, the world; the seemingly endless list of cured pork products that come under the general term for cured meats, *salumi*, including Parma ham; and the incomparable handmade pastas such as tortellini and fettuccine.

The *salumi* of Emilia-Romagna are truly exceptional, and each town feels it produces the best. Frankly, it's hard to go wrong! *Salumi* are usually offered as part of the antipasto (well worth sampling), but they also make a great sandwich for lunch on the go or a picnic.

The homemade, egg-rich pastas of Emilia-Romagna are legendary. The soft wheat grown on the fertile plains of the Po River, Italy's wheat belt, led to the creation of this elevated art form. Today Emilia-Romagna cannot grow enough wheat to satisfy the need, so some is imported from Canada and the United States. The rituals of hand-stretching, rolling, and filling the dough have been practiced for centuries, and both the quality and variety produced here are extraordinary. The myriad shapes and fillings—and even the names—differ from town to town, and they can overwhelm the uninitiated. Take heart—no one can truly decipher all the vagaries of pasta in Emilia-Romagna, so jump in anytime! (See Menu Primer A to Z: *Aceto balsamico*, *Formaggio*, *Parmigiano-reggiano*, *Pasta*, and *Salumi* and Market Buying Tips: *Aceto balsamico*, *Formaggi/ Parmigiano-reggiano*, *Pasta*, and *Salumi*.)

Baccalà alla bolognese (bah kah LAH ah lah boh loh NYAY zay). Dried salt cod cooked with a sauce of lemon, garlic, and parsley. (See Menu Primer A to Z: *Baccalà*.)

Bollito misto (bol LEE toh MEES toh). Literally, a "boiled mixture." Actually, it's a "mixed bag" of meats. Here in Emilia-Romagna, the meats range from pork sausage, pig's foot, tongue, beef, and veal to capon. The meats are sided with two sauces, one a piquant green, *salsa verde* (SAL sah VAYR day), made with capers, and the other a fruit chutney called *mostarda* (mos TAHR dah). (See Menu Primer A to Z: *Bollito misto* and *Mostarda*.)

Brodetto (braw DET toh). Fish stew from Romagna's coast on the Adriatic Sea. Ingredients vary according to the fish available and to the proclivities of the cook. (See Menu Primer A to Z: *Brodetto*.)

Cappelletti (kahp pel LET tee), or *tortellini* (tor tel LEE nee), *in brodo* (een BRAW doh). Fresh, handmade filled pasta in a rich poultry or meat stock. Noodle soup made in heaven!

Capretto (kah PRET toh). Baby goat, or kid, which when listed as *alla piacentina* (pyah chen TEE nah) is simmered in a white wine sauce.

Ciambella (chee am BEL lah). A ring (or sometimes a loaf) of pastry often flavored with anise and lemon peel, filled (or not!) with jam. Back in the seventeenth century, the ring shape made the cakes easy to sell in the marketplace because vendors carried them strung on long sticks.

Coppa (KOHP pah). A specialty of Piacenza, salt-cured boneless ham, often a part of the antipasto platter.

Costoletta alla bolognese (kos toh LET tah ah lah boh loh NYAY zay). Bologna-style is breaded, then fried in butter. It's next covered with ham and Parmesan and quickly melted in the oven, then topped with either meat sauce or tomato sauce. (See Menu Primer A to Z: *Vitello: alla bolognese.*)

Cotechino (kot eh KEE noh). This is yet another of the delicious cured pork sausages of the region. The filling is coarsely ground and spiced according to each town's recipe. The sausage is steamed or poached and usually served with mashed potatoes, lentils, or braised beans.

Culatello (koo lah TEHL loh). From Parma, this rare and costly ham is derived from the leanest part of the rump of the pig. This highly revered product is often served with a delicious fried bread called *torta fritta* (TOR tah FREET tah).

Mortadella (mor tah DEHL lah). This is the magnificent, smooth-textured, torpedo-shaped sausage of Bologna. It's the original—and by far the finest "baloney"—made with cubes of fat, black peppercorns, other spices, and often pistachio nuts scattered throughout. In Emilia-Romagna, it's served in bite-size cubes as part of the antipasto as well as sliced.

Passatelli in brodo (pahs sah TEHL lee een BRAW doh). These are squiggly-shaped dumplings from Romagna made from cheese, bread crumbs, nutmeg, lemon peel, and eggs. They are served in a rich poultry broth that's usually made from a capon.

Pasta

- *Anolini* (ahn oh LEE nee). From Parma, rich meat-filled pasta, circular in shape, sauced, or served in delicious broth, often made from a capon.
- *Cappellacci* (kahp pel LAH chee). These large, fresh pasta (the same cap shape as tortellini) are filled with sweet orange squash and *parmigiano-reggiano* and are usually topped with just a sage-butter sauce and *parmigiano-reggiano*.
- *Cappelletti* (kahp pel LET tee). So named in Romagna. In Emilia, they're *tortellini*. Resembling little caps, these filled pastas are said to imitate

the hats of Spanish soldiers. Depending on the town in which they are made, they can be meat- or cheese-filled, but usually they contain pork, pork sausage, mortadella, and *parmigiano-reggiano* or ricotta.

- *Garganelli* (gahr gahn EHL lee). These are hollow, ribbed cylinders made with egg pasta. They're shaped over a dowel, then ribbed by running the dowel over a ridged board. Talk about labor-intensive!

- *Gramigna* (grah MEE nyah). This is another homemade egg pasta, made with a hand-operated machine that extrudes the dough and creates short, wiggly lengths of pasta with a hole running through the middle. They're traditionally served with braised sausage.

- *Lasagne* (lah ZAHN nyay). In Emilia-Romagna, this familiar dish rises to new heights. The broad, flat strips of homemade pasta (often *lasagne verdi* [VEYR dee], green pasta made with spinach), are layered with the region's sensational *ragù* (rah GOO), or meat sauce, béchamel, and a dusting of *parmigiano-reggiano*, then baked.

- *Maltagliati* (mahl tahl YAH tee). Literally, "badly cut," this pasta is cut into uneven shapes and used in soups and other rustic dishes.

- *Pappardelle* (pahp pahr DEHL lee). Wide ribbons (five-eighths of an inch!) of handmade egg pasta that are usually served with the classic meat sauce, *ragù* or *ragù bolognese*. (See below.)

- *Pasticcio* (pahs TEE chyoh). It's the word for pie,

but here it indicates a pasta layered with *ragù*, meatballs, and sweet custard, baked in a piecrust. This is a lavish dish, of the type favored by the aristocracy of the sixteenth and seventeenth centuries, when sweet and savory tastes were intermingled throughout the menus of the upper crust.

- *Strozzapreti* (stroh tsah PREH tee). The literal translation is "priest stranglers." The pasta looks like twisted strands of tagliatelle (see below), rolled thicker than most local pastas and meant to be very filling. All the better to fill up the village priest, who appeared regularly for a free meal, as the pasta course preceded the more expensive meat course! (In Romagna, pasta was such an integral part of life that it was even a means of making social commentary.)
- *Tagliarini* (tahl lyar REE nee) or tagliolinè (tahl lyoh LEE nee). Very thin versions of tagliatelle.
- *Tagliatelle* (tahl yah TEL lay). Long, ribbonlike (three-eighths an inch) strips of handmade pasta dough. According to legend, they were first created by a Bolognese cook who was very taken with the long blond tresses of Lucrezia Borgia. The pasta is traditionally topped with *ragù* (rah GOO) or Bolognese meat sauce, a rich, slow-cooked sauce containing onion, celery, carrot, and various meats, including beef and pork, as well as wine, tomatoes, and often milk.
- *Tortelli* (tor TEL lee). Rectangles or squares of pasta stuffed with various fillings, often vegeta-

bles and cheeses, such as mild greens, ricotta, *parmigiano-reggiano,* and a little nutmeg or cabbage and potatoes flavored with onion and garlic. They're usually served topped with butter and Parmesan.

- *Tortellini* (tor tel LEE nee). The mother of all filled pastas, and the inhabitants of each town will vehemently uphold their version of the filling as the best. In Bologna, turkey, pork, veal, mortadella, prosciutto, and *parmigiano-reggiano* are essential. Other variations can include chicken or capon and cheese, while some are meatless, filled just with cheeses, herbs, and spices. The pasta is cut into small squares, filled, and folded over to make a triangle; then the two opposing ends are twisted and pressed together to form the traditional shape. (Remember, this is all done by hand!) Generally served either in broth or simply, with butter and more *parmigiano.* Legends differ as to the origins of the shape; one version adored by the lusty natives tells of a time when the gods still walked the earth. A humble Bolognese innkeeper playing host to the goddess Venus was enthralled by the accidental sight of her exquisite navel and rushed to the kitchen to create a pasta modeled after this wonder!

- *Tortelloni* (tor tel LO nee). The much larger (and thereby somewhat less labor intensive) cousin of tortellini, usually stuffed with ricotta, egg, Parmesan, parsley, and nutmeg.

Piadina (pyah DEE nah). The ancient flatbread of Romagna, traditionally baked over a fire on a thick terra cotta stone has been reinvented as the fast-food flatbread of Romagna, similar to a flour tortilla. It's served at snack stands as well as with meals. Traditional fillings include prosciutto, salami, and sautéed greens or the delicious cheese of Romagna, *squaquerone* (skwah kweh ROH neh).

Prosciutto (pro SHOOT toh). Ham. *Prosciutto crudo* (pro SHOOT toh KROO doh) refers to salted, air-cured ham. It's also called *prosciutto di Parma,* which is one of the best known of the cured hams, from the regions surrounding Parma in Emilia-Romagna. *Prosciutto di Parma* is made from pork thigh meat taken from pigs who, by law, are raised in specific areas around Parma. These pampered pigs are fed the whey from the *parmigiano-reggiano*–making process. Hams are cured with salt and aged in the (evidently!) rarified local air. (See Menu Primer A to Z: *Prosciutto.*)

Prosciutto e melone (pro SHOOT toh ay mey LOH nay). This is the classic appetizer using *prosciutto di Parma,* no doubt the most famous of the cured hams from Emilia. This satiny-textured ham is served sliced thin and wrapped around a slice of melon, usually cantaloupe.

Ragù, Ragù bolognese (rah GOO boh loh NYAY say). Meat sauces are found throughout Italy, but the ragù of Bologna is the most famous in the country. It's made with pork and beef, which are well browned along with carrots, celery, and onion, then long-simmered with wine, tomato paste, milk, and cream.

Ribollita (ree bohl LEE tah), a.k.a. *minestra di pane* (mee NES tra dee PAH nay). Literaly, "reboiled." This soup is made in large quantities, then reheated on the second day, causing it to thicken. It is made with vegetables, often onion, carrots, celery, garlic, and cabbage, and broth thickened with stale bread and laced with olive oil.

Salame da sugo (sahl LAH may dah SOO go). A traditional regional dish of aged pork sausage that's crumbled and served with mashed potatoes.

Tacchino al cardinale (tahk KEE noh ahl kahr dee NAH leh). Turkey cooked with prosciutto and *parmigiano*. This preparation, usually reserved for a whole roast capon, is traditionally served for Christmas, but in this area it's made with turkey (*tacchino*) breast.

Torta di riso (TOR tah dee REE zoh). The rice pudding of Modena, flavored with candied citron or almonds, is baked and sliced like a cake. The starchy arborio rice grown in the region and used in risotto is also the basis for this dessert.

Torta di tagliarini (TOR tah dee tahl lyah REE nee). This is an exceptionally good tart, with a crunchy texture. A sweet pastry base is filled with the thin strands of pasta called tagliarini that are mixed with toasted almonds, candied fruit, eggs, sugar, flour, and liqueur. The recipe appeared at banquets during the Renaissance, a time when serving pasta with sugar was a sign of exalted status, and to this day the dish is still served at special occasions.

Zampone (zahm POH nay). Pork sausage, a specialty from the town of Modena in Emilia-Romagna. The sausage is stuffed into a casing made from a pig's foot, cooked, and served with lentils. The dish is served as a main course, especially on New Year's Day, to insure good luck throughout the year.

FRIULI–VENEZIA GIULIA

Bordering on the former Yugoslavia, Austria, Veneto, and the Adriatic Sea, the combined region of Friuli–Venezia Giulia has had its share of war and changing boundaries. But in spite of their history of hardship, the people of this region are known for their warmth and hospitality. There's no better symbol of this than the *fogolar*, the traditional open hearth that is a focal point in both restaurants and homes of the region. The multiethnic tradition has led to interesting contrasts in the cuisine. Humble foods of the peasants of Friuli are found next to the more sophisticated table of Venezia Giulia, which tells of strong Slavic, Austrian, and Hungarian influences.

Grains such as cornmeal and barley, legumes, vegetables, and cheese dominated the diet of the poor. Smoke from the fire was actually a major contributor of flavor, as in the local *ricotta affumicata* or smoked ricotta, and the cured, then smoked, specialty of Friuli, *prosciutto affumicato*. Barnyard animals, predominantly pigs and geese, were raised, and the famous *prosciutto di San Daniele,* which many think is the best ham in Italy, is made in the hills of San Daniele. Among the area's Jewish population, goose products were once substituted for the flavorful pork products (traditionally forbidden to Jews), and today some of these specialties can be found in shops.

Hungarian goulash, the famous beef stew, locally called *gulyas,* is a favorite here, and it's cooked with onions, herbs, and paprika much like its progenitor. Desserts reflect the Austrian sweet tooth; strudel (called *strucolo*) is a favorite on the *dolce* menu.

Brodetto (braw DET toh). Fish soup or stew. (See Menu Primer A to Z: *Brodetto.*)

Brovada (braw VAH dah). Evidence of the centuries-old *cucina povera* of the region, this humble dish consists of turnips that have been fermented with grape skins (leftover from the wine-making process) for a month, then grated. The grated turnips are cooked and served with pork sausage.

Cialzone (chyal TSOH neh). If ever there was a dish that's hard to pin down it's *cialzons,* or *cjalsons,* or *cjarsons* (you begin to get the picture). *Cialzone* can be either gnocchi (potato dumplings) or pasta stuffed with over forty ingredients (which vary widely), including spinach, onions, potatoes, chocolate, lemon, cinnamon, raisins, and smoked ricotta. They are served with melted butter, and are absolutely delicious!

Frico or *fricco* (FREE koh). These fried cheese fritters (some include apple along with the cheese) are seasoned with salt and pepper and served as an appetizer. They are made with the local cow's milk cheese, *latteria* (lah teh REE yah).

Gnocchi (NYOH kee). Potato dumplings, made with just potato and flour, are commonly served in the region, but other versions may be made with bread crumbs, *di pane* (PAH nay), or stuffed with prunes, *di susina* (soo ZEE nah) (the Austrian influence again), or with winter squash, *di zucca* (TSOOK koh), and topped with a grating of the local smoked ricotta.

Gubana (goo BAH nah). A traditional pastry, which for centuries was made with a yeast dough into a puffy, spiral shape and filled with nuts, candied fruits, and liqueur. Today you are more likely to be served a lighter, flakier pastry.

Gulyas (GOOL yahs). This hearty beef stew, better known as goulash, is cooked with onions, herbs, and paprika.

Iota (EEOH tah). This is a soup typical of Trieste, where the Austrian influence is still strong. It contains white beans, bacon, cabbage or turnips, and sometimes polenta (cornmeal).

Minestra d'orzo e fagioli (mee NES trah D'OR zoh ay fah JOH lee). This hearty soup is made from barley and beans, usually the local beans known as *carnia*.

Musett (moo ZET). Another fine *salumi* particular to the region, this is a cooked pork sausage, often spiced with cinnamon and coriander.

Pasta

This is a region where the Austrian influence is strong. Cialzone *can* be made with pasta—or gnocchi—and there are some squash-filled ravioli.

- *Ravioli di zucca* (rah VYOH lee dee TSOOK kah). Squash-filled pasta—sometimes made with potato dough.

Polenta e salsiccia (poh LEHN tah ay sahl SEET chah). Polenta, which is ground cornmeal, is the preferred starch in much of the region. Here it is paired with sausages for a hearty dish appropriate to the harsh climate.

Prosciutto crudo di San Daniele (pro SHOOT toh KROO doh dee sahn dahn YEH leh). An outstanding cured ham of Friuli. Thin-sliced, it will be served as part of the antipasto, but the sweet/salty ham is also used on sandwiches and to flavor sauces and other dishes. (See Menu Primer A to Z: *Prosciutto.*)

Strucolo (stroo KOH loh). The influence of former Austro-Hungarian rulers remains today in Friuli–Venezia Giulia, especially in the pastries. The Friuli versions of this delicious strudel contain either ricotta and raisins or apples.

LAZIO

Much of the region of Lazio consists of serene, pastoral farmland, hills, lakes, and the beautiful coastline of the Mare Tirreno, but at its heart lies the incomparable Roma! And whether you're strolling through the streets, gazing at world-famous monuments, touring the Vatican, or eating dinner, history surrounds you.

The Romans do pay respect to their culinary heritage; improvisation is not likely at the table. The *cucina* is based on the marketplace, a tradition as old as the Forum, that ancient market that served as the nerve center of ancient Rome. The market tradition remains today—the season's fresh produce you spot at the morning markets appears on the evening menu. In springtime, exquisite peas and artichokes are showcased in classic dishes, and *abbacchio,* baby lamb, appears on cue at Easter celebrations. Romans adhere to daily traditions as well. Fish is served, of course, on Friday, and often it's salt cod, *baccalà*. Gnocchi (potato dumplings) show up on Thursdays, tripe on Saturdays, and a special meal is served on Sundays, perhaps homemade pasta or the treat of meat, usually pork or lamb. The choice cheese is pecorino, sheep's cheese, both fresh and mild, as well as the sharply flavored aged variety that's used to grate into your pasta dish.

Eating in Rome is a lusty affair, and there is much emphasis on enjoying the pleasures of both food and wine. No spartan diet this—fat (from the region's gutsy olive oil) and salt are evident in prodigious amounts. Salt was such an important commodity to the Romans in ancient times that they constructed a road called Via Salaria, or Salt Road, to provide access to the salt harvested from the Adriatic Sea. But it would be a shame to come to Rome and not indulge; perhaps that's where that old adage comes from: "When in Rome . . ."!

Agnello (ahn YEL loh). Lamb is the meat most commonly found in Lazio, where it's prepared simply, usually roasted with fresh herbs like rosemary and sage. Rome's most celebrated dish is *abbacchio* (ahb BAH kyoh), a one-month-old-baby lamb, traditionally roasted with garlic and rosemary, sage, and sometimes anchovies. It's the quintessential dish served for Easter to welcome in the spring and celebrate rebirth. (See Menu Primer A to Z: *Agnello*.)

Anguille (ahn GWEEL leh). These are the eels from Lago di Bolsena that are so highly prized. The tradition in Rome is to eat the eels along with the legendary wine Est! Est! Est! (See Beverages A to Z: *Est! Est! Est!*.)

Bruschetta (broos KET tah). The original garlic toast and, by far, the best! In late fall, when the freshly pressed olive oil is released, the tradition of toasting bread over the open fire, then drizzling it generously with the spicy new oil continues. Garlic rubbed on the toasted bread was an early, essential addition. Various other toppings such as tomatoes with a leaf of basil have followed.

Carciofi alla Giudia (kahr CHOH fee ah lah joo DAY ah). Artichokes, Jewish-style. In spring, when young artichokes are available, they're deep-fried until they're crisp on the outside, but still creamy and succulent on the inside, and flattened and fried again. The end result looks like a flower. They're a tradition from the Roman Jewish ghetto, an area that remains a distinct neighborhood today. Because of their dietary restrictions, the Jews created a number of excellent dishes with the wonderful vegetables from the surrounding area.

Carciofi alla romana (kahr CHOH fee ah lah roh MAHN nah). Artichokes, Roman-style, are another of the pleasures of springtime. Tender young artichokes are trimmed but left whole, stuffed with the wild mint of the region, along with garlic and parsley, and slow-cooked in olive oil until meltingly tender.

Coda alla vaccinara (KO dah ah lah vah chee NAH rah). Oxtail stew. A delicious, slow-cooked specialty found especially in Lazio, it's flavored with carrots, onion, celery, parsley, and a little prosciutto, and cooked in wine with bay leaves and tomatoes.

Fave al guanciale (FAH vay ahl gwan CHAH leh). Fava beans are a type of broad bean that are best eaten when very young, in May and June in Rome. In this dish they are stewed along with some hog's jowl, or *guanciale*, onion, and tomatoes. Fava beans are also found in salads or paired with pecorino and served as the cheese course after a meal.

Fritto misto alla romana (FREET toh MEES toh ah lah roh MAH nah). Rome's version of "mixed fry" generally is meat-based, with pork or lamb, organ meats, and vegetables, all of which are battered and deep-fried. (See Menu Primer A to Z: *Fritto misto.*)

Gnocchi alla romana or *di semolella* (NYOH kee ah lah roh MAH nah or dee seh moh LEHL lah). The Roman version of dumplings differs from those of other regions. Here, disk-shaped dumplings are made of semolina, eggs, milk, butter, and Parmesan, topped with more butter and *parmigiano*, and baked in the oven.

Insalata di mare (een sah LAH tah dee MAH ray). This cold seafood salad is served wherever there is seacoast, but in the southern regions such as Lazio, it's usually accompanied by vegetables that have been preserved in vinegar, along with olives and capers. (See Menu Primer A to Z: *Insalata di mare*.)

Pasta

- *Bucatini all'amatriciana* (ahl ah maht tree CHYAH nah). One of the many pasta traditions that tell the history of the region. From the pastoral lands of Amatrice comes the centuries-old dish made by shepherds with the ingredients on hand: bucatini, the easily attained thick, hollow spaghetti, pecorino (sheep's milk cheese), *guanciale* (hog's jowl), and lots of black pepper. After his second voyage to the New World, Columbus returned with (among other novelties) the tomato, and eventually this dish took on a new guise. The version with the addition of the tomato is now favored, but the original (and I think superior) one might be listed as *pasta alla gricia* (GREE chyah) and should be sampled if possible. (See Menu Primer A to Z: *Pasta/Salse: All'amatriciana*.)
- *Fettuccine maestose al burro* (fet too CHEE nay mah eys TOH seh ahl BOOR roh). Better known as fettuccine Alfredo (ahl FRAY doh), this dish was created in Rome and with typical abandon is made with plenty of butter, Parmesan, and sometimes cream. (See Comfort Foods: Pasta.)
- *Penne all'arrabbiata* (PEYN nay ahl ah rah BYAH tah). Quill-shaped dried pasta, cooked in "angry" sauce made with lots of the hot red chili peppers

that are a signature of southern Italian cooking. The dish also includes bacon, tomatoes, garlic, and pecorino.

- *Spaghetti alla carbonara* (kar boh NAH rah). A rich spaghetti dish, known far beyond the borders of Italy. It's made with *guanciale* (pork jowl) or *pancetta* (unsmoked Italian bacon), garlic, hot chili peppers, olive oil, pecorino, black pepper, and egg yolks that are mixed into the hot pasta to enrich the dish. (See Menu Primer A to Z: *Pasta/ Salse: alla carbonara.*)

Porchetta (por KET tah). Roasted suckling pig, flavored with garlic, rosemary, and black pepper. In Lazio, this dish is often featured at Sunday dinner. It also appears at roadside food stalls, where the succulent meat is served in sandwiches. (See Menu Primer A to Z: *Porchetta.*)

Saltimbocca alla romana (sahl teem BOK kah ah lah roh MAH nah). Literally, saltimbocca means "jump in the mouth," a term that aptly describes the dish, a specialty of the region. Veal scallops are layered with thinly sliced prosciutto and fresh sage leaves, which can either be rolled or left flat and secured with a toothpick. Either way, they are then browned in butter and simmered in wine.

Stracciatella (strah chah TEHL lah). A favorite soup in Lazio, *stracciatella alla romana* (strah chah TEHL lah ah lah ro MAHN nah) consists of hot chicken broth to which a mixture of eggs, semolina, and grated romano cheese are added at the last minute, then swirled "egg drop"–style. The heat of the soup cooks the egg. (See Menu Primer A to Z: *Stracciatella*.)

Suppli di riso (soop LEE dee REE zoh) or *suppli al telefono* (tey LEY foh noh). These are delicious rice croquettes in which cooked rice is mixed with Parmesan, then allowed to cool. Balls of rice are formed and stuffed with a cube of (usually) mozzarella, dipped in beaten egg, rolled in bread crumbs, and deep-fried. Before eating, pull them apart with your hands to see the melted cheese stretch like a mass of telephone wires. They will appear on the antipasto menu.

Torta di ricotta (TOR tah dee ree KOHT tah). This is the wonderful, light Italian take on cheesecake, made with the local ricotta.

Tortino di riso (tor TEE noh dee REE zoh). This is essentially rice pudding. Sweet "cakes" are made of rice that's cooked with raisins, milk, sugar, and lemon, then mixed with eggs and baked, usually in individual molds. It's often on the menu in cafés, where you might want to stop for a *caffè* and a little something sweet.

LIGURIA

Liguria is the thin strip of land that's known as the Italian Riviera. It's protected from the frigid north winds by the Apennines and Alps and bathed by the warm breezes off the Ligurian Sea. Although much of the land is hilly and not suitable for growing wheat or for pastureland, the hospitable climate produces fine vegetables and fruits, wonderfully aromatic fresh herbs like basil and marjoram, and olive oil that's fragrant and light. The basil and oil turn up in Genoa's gastronomic gift to the world—pesto. Delicious flatbread known as focaccia is topped with the olive oil and the ubiquitous fresh herbs.

The diet of the Ligurians is largely vegetarian and probably the healthiest in Italy. Vegetables are invariably stuffed with herbs, cheeses, and nuts, and these dishes will be tagged *ripieno*, or *farcito*. Fresh seafood and dried salt cod are more prevalent than meat, most of which comes from barnyard animals such as chickens and rabbits. Wines are produced in abundance from vineyards near the borders of neighboring Piemonte and Toscana, two of the largest wine-producing regions in Italy.

Acciughe marinate (ah CHOO geh mahr ee NAH teh). These are the fresh anchovies that are marinated in lemon juice rather than the salt-cured or *sotto sale* (SOT toh SAH leh) anchovies.

Arrosto alla genovese (ah ROHS toh ah lah jen oh VAY zay). This is Genoa's beef or veal pot roast with onion gravy. It can also include carrots, celery, tomatoes, mushrooms, and wine.

Baccalà alla genovese (bah kah LAH ah lah jen oh VAY zay). When salt cod appears on the menu in Liguria, it's usually cooked with fresh tomato sauce and herbs. (See Menu Primer A to Z: *Baccalà.*)

Burrida (boor REE doh). This is the wonderful fish stew of Liguria, made with either fresh fish or dried salt cod, *baccalà*. It is sometimes prepared with dried vegetables as onions, garlic, carrots, and tomatoes.

Cappon magro (kahp PONE MAH groh). Literally, "lean capon." This is a Ligurian specialty (its name is actually a play on words because it's a meatless dish) and a tradition on Christmas Eve and other feast days. It is an elaborate pyramid of poached fish, shrimp, lobster, and oysters layered with vegetables in a sauce of herbs, pine nuts, and capers. The "real" capon is served on Christmas day.

Cima alla genovese (CHEE mah ah lah jen oh VAY zay). This is stuffed breast of veal, filled with organ meats, herbs, veal pâté, peas, pine nuts, and cheese (pecorino or parmigiano). It's rolled up in a cloth, boiled, then chilled and served thinly sliced.

Coniglio (koh NEE lyoh). A specialty of Liguria, rabbit often appears on menus in the region, cooked in various ways using the local herbs and white wine. When prepared *in umido* (OO mee doh), it's braised with herbs and spices, pine nuts, and white wine.

Farinata (fahr ee NAH tah). This is a delicious crepe made from chickpeas, baked in pizza ovens, and found in fry shops called *friggitorie*. They are worth seeking out but are usually available only in the morning.

Frittata (freet TAH tah). Here in Liguria, these pan-fried omelettes are filled with vegetables such as zucchini and sometimes with sardines or anchovies. (See Menu Primer A to Z: *Frittata*.)

Mesciua (mes CHOO ah). This is a soup made with the ubiquitous chickpeas, the grain called *farro*, beans, and pepper and enriched with olive oil.

Pasta

- *Corzetti* (kor TZET tee). These are the traditional handmade pasta of Liguria, either cut into disks with a decorative wooden stamp or into figure-eight shapes. They are served *alla polce-verasca* (pol chey veyr AZ kah), a sauce of pine nuts (or sometimes walnuts), herbs, and butter.
- *Pansoti* (pahn SOH tee). This stuffed pasta is filled with cheese and some type of green and served with walnut sauce.
- *Ravioli di magro* (rah VYOH lee dee MAH groh). These are filled with ricotta and wild herbs and sauced with another tradition of the region, walnut sauce, made much like pesto, but with walnuts added.
- *Trofie* (TRO fyeh). They are a squiggly-shaped,

homemade pasta served with green beans, potatoes, and pesto.

Pasta alla genovese (PAH stah ah lah jen oh VAY zay). This is not pasta at all but the sponge cake, better known by its French name, *génoise*, that actually originated in Genoa.

Pesto (PEY stoh). This vibrant green sauce of Genoa is adored by food lovers around the world, and it doesn't get any better than here in Liguria. Pesto is traditionally made by pounding fresh basil leaves in a stone mortar together with garlic, pine nuts, pecorino, Parmesan, and olive oil. (The name comes from the verb *pestare*, which means "to pound.") This highly flavored sauce is used to flavor pastas such as lasagna and *trenette* (trey NEHT teh), a thin, flat pasta, and to perk up soups, especially minestrone. (See Menu Primer A to Z: *Pesto*.)

Sardenaira (sahr dey NAY rah) or *pissadella* (pee sah DEHL lah). This is the signature pizza of the Ligurian Riviera, with anchovies, tomatoes, onion, and olives.

Scabecio (skah BAY chyoh). Fish is fried, then marinated or pickled in a sauce of vinegar, onion, garlic, and fresh herbs.

Scorzanera (skor tsahn AY rah). Salsify root is delicious when served deep-fried, when it's similar to french fries, or braised.

Torta pasqualina (TOR tah pahs kwa LEE nah). "Easter tart." Traditionally made of thirty-three paper-thin layers of pastry, which stand for the thirty-three years of Christ's life, they are stuffed with artichokes, chard, ricotta, and hard-boiled eggs. On nonfeast days, the tart may be made with as few as four layers of pastry and filled with different vegetables, including fava beans.

Triglia alla genovese (TREE lyah ah lah jen oh VAY zay). This is red mullet that's baked in a sauce of fennel seeds, tomato paste, white wine, and capers.

Tuccu (TOO koo), or *tocco* (TOH koh). A general term that refers to sauces, all of which are used on pasta but made of different ingredients. When designated *de nuxe* (dey NOOX), *tuccu* is a creamy sauce of walnuts, garlic, bread, and sometimes pecorino or *parmigiano* cheese. *Tuccu di carne* (dee KAHR nay) is meat sauce, and *tuccu di funghi* (FOON ghee) is mushroom sauce.

LOMBARDIA (LOMBARDY)

At the base of the Alps, tucked between Piemonte, Emilia-Romagna, Veneto, and Trentino Alto–Adige, lies the wealthiest region in Italy, Lombardia. At its nerve center is Milano, a big, bustling city whose people are industrious, creative, and very influential. Politics are as much a part of the scene today as they were in the tumultuous past centuries, during which the area was constantly buffeted by changes in rulers.

The region is made up of fertile plains to the south, the beautiful lake district (Lake Como has been a playground for the smart set for centuries), and mountains (the Alps) to the north. This variety in terrain gives Lombardia a wide range of food products and cooking styles and allows for many gastronomic treats. The southern plains are fertile, and rice, corn, and wheat are plentiful. Risotto, an excellent first course in Lombardia, is made from the region's special short- to medium-grain rices, whose texture and starch content yield a perfect al dente grain with creamy sauce that makes itself. Corn is made into polenta, the food that once staved off the peasants' cold and hunger and now appears on trendy menus throughout the world. Excellent handmade pastas with unusual fillings are made here, too.

From the pastures where cattle are raised come butter, cream, and extraordinary cheeses (including the delicious blue-veined gorgonzola and the wonderful taleggio), which all play major roles in the region's specialties. Veal dishes are also exemplary here. Osso buco, Cotoletta alla milanese, and veal scallops cooked with marsala are local specialties that are famous throughout most of the world. Lakes provide lovely fresh fish, most of which have unfamiliar names but deserve investigation.

Delectable traditional desserts are found mainly in pastry shops, not usually on restaurant menus. *Panettone,* the classic Milanese yeast cake studded with raisins and candied fruit is traditionally made for Christmas, and an unusual crunchy cake made from pasta, *torta di tagliatelle*, are among the special items worth seeking out.

Asparagi alla milanese (ahs PAH rah jee ah lah meel ahn AY zay). It's asparagus boiled, then topped with Parmesan, butter—and a fried egg!

Bollito misto (bol LEE toh MEES toh). Meats are a major part of the region's diet, so it's no surprise that the "mixed boiled meat" dish (here it typically includes beef, veal, tongue, pork, and sausage), which is served with various sauces, is frequently on the menu. (See Menu Primer A to Z: *Bollito misto*.)

Bresaola (bray SAYOH lah). An exceptional specialty of the northern valley of Valtellina, this *salumi* is made from a whole beef filet that has been cured in salt and air-dried. It can appear either as part of the antipasto or as a main dish, *secondo*, sliced very thin and served atop a bed of arugula, dressed with olive oil and pepper and topped with *parmigiano-reggiano*.

Busecca (boo SEK kah). This is the tripe soup that's made in Milano. Tripe, the stomach of animals—sheep, oxen, and cows, is very popular in Italy. It's made tender by slow-cooking, and it's flavored with tomato sauce, vegetables, and beans and topped with Parmesan. (See Menu Primer A to Z: *Trippa*.)

Casoeula (kahs oh eh OO lah). This is a stew made with pork sausage, other cuts of pork, and vegetables (usually cabbage) and served over polenta.

Cotoletta alla milanese (kot oh LET tah ah lah meel ahn AY zay). This is a veal cutlet, or sometimes a chop, that's dipped in beaten egg, dredged in bread crumbs, and fried in butter. This method is borrowed from the Milanesi and used worldwide, with many interpretations.

Insalata alla russa (een sah LAH tah ah lah ROOS sah). A "Russian salad," so named because it consists of several ingredients like potatoes, peas, and beans that are just tossed together rather than composed. The inference is not exactly a compliment—in Italy, a messy room is referred to as a "real Russia."

Mascarpone (mahs kahr POH nay). A wonderful rich and creamy cheese made in Lombardia. (See Menu Primer A to Z: *Mascarpone* and Market Buying Tips: *Formaggi: Mascarpone*.)

Minestrone (meen ehs TROH nay). A mixed vegetable soup. In Lombardia, it's cooked with beans and rice. (See Menu Primer A to Z: *Minestrone*.)

Osso buco (AWS soh BOO koh). Braised veal shanks, slow-cooked with onion, carrot, celery, tomatoes, broth, and wine. The dish is often found on menus in Lombardia. (See Menu Primer A to Z: *Osso buco*.)

Pasta

- *Agnolini* (ahn nyoh LEE nee). This is fresh, hand-made pasta, filled with meat, Parmesan, and spices.

- *Cansonsei* (kahn sohn say). Pasta filled with various meats, usually including sausage, vegetables, and cheese. They are made and prepared in various ways according to the town but can be served in broth or sauced with just melted butter.

- *Pizzoccheri* (peets oh KAY ree). Pasta made of buckwheat cut into strips—*tagliatelle* (tahl yah TEL lay)—and served with potatoes, cabbage, butter, and Parmesan.

- *Tortelli di zucca* (tor TEL lee dee TSOOK kah). Fresh pasta stuffed with the local pumpkin or winter squash, *mostarda* (a kind of chutney), and finely ground amaretti (almond cookies) and served with butter, sage leaves,. and Parmesan.

Piccata al marsala (peek KAH tah ahl mahr SAH lah). Veal scallops, sautéed in butter, then simmered in marsala, and served over *risotto alla milanese* (ree ZOHT toh ah lah meel ahn AY zay). This is another veal dish that's been adopted and somewhat reinterpreted all over the world.

Polenta. (See Menu Primer A to Z: *Polenta*.)

Riso al salto (REE zoh ahl SAHL toh). Leftover *risotto alla milanese* (ree ZOHT toh ah lah meel ahn AY zay) does not go to waste—it's formed into a patty and fried in butter until crisp.

Risotto alla milanese (ree ZOHT toh meel ahn AY zay). Short-grained (usually the locally grown arborio) rice is sautéed with onions and beef marrow in butter, then hot stock is slowly added to the pan in batches and the mixture is stirred until the rice has reached the proper creamy (not sticky!) consistency. Saffron is added to both flavor and color the rice. It is then enriched with a handful of *parmigiano-reggiano* and a little more butter. The beautiful amber-gold hue and the exquisite texture of a properly made *risotto alla milanese* make this simple dish one of Italy's most glorious creations. (See Menu Primer A to Z: *Risotto* and Market Buying Tips: *Riso*.)

Salami di Milano (sah LAH mee dee mee LAH noh). The fine-textured salami of Milan is made of pork, garlic, and assorted spices. You'll often find it as part of the antipasto.

Sciatt (SHYAHT). These are deep-fried buckwheat fritters filled with cheese. They are likely to appear on the antipasto platter, especially in the northern part of Lombardia.

Zuppa pavese (TSOOP pah pah VAY zay). Soup from the city of Pavia. First, a piece of fried bread is place in a soup bowl. An egg is broken onto the bread, and then steaming hot, rich broth is poured over the top to cook the egg. The soup is topped with Parmesan, chopped parsley, and pepper.

LE MARCHE (THE MARCHES)

Difficult access to the region of Le Marche because of the Apennines, which separate it from its neighbors, Emilia-Romagna, Toscana, Umbria, Lazio, and Abruzzo, may explain why it is relatively unknown outside the country. The other boundary is the Adriatic coastline, and it is here that tourists come to enjoy the beaches. Other than this strip of flat land, which can get crowded, the remainder of the landmass consists of mountains and hills, where quiet prevails.

The coast's culinary creations from the bounty of the Adriatic are among the best, and the local *brodetto,* or fish stew, is superb. As might be expected, versions differ from town to town. The hills and mountains supply olives, grapes (the famous white wine verdicchio comes from here), mushrooms and black truffles, and meats and cheeses. The traditional cuisine has been carefully preserved, and many of the local specialties date back to Roman times.

Brodetto (braw DET toh). This is the name given to fish stews that are found all along the Adriatic coast, but the best is here in Le Marche. Recipes differ, but, in general, the northern version uses thirteen different fish (mullet is an essential), onion, garlic, herbs, olive oil, and vinegar and is ladled over a slice of plain garlic-rubbed bread. Southern cooks flour the fish (of which there are a mere nine types) and add saffron and a slice of toasted bread. Some cooks prefer to use only one type of fish, such as the Adriatic sole. To each his own! (See Menu Primer A to Z: *Brodetto*.)

Coniglio (koh NEE lyoh). Rabbit turns up frequently in the region and is prepared in various ways. The cooks here seem to have a penchant for stuffing things, and *coniglio all'anconetana* (ahn koh neh TAH nah) has a bread stuffing flavored with garlic, prosciutto, fennel, nutmeg, lemon, and olive oil. When prepared *in porchetta* (por KET tah), it is stuffed (often with wild fennel, garlic, and pancetta) and baked in a wood-burning oven in the same manner as the *porchetta*, the small suckling pig. (See Menu Primer A to Z: *Coniglio*.)

Olive ascolane (oh LEE veh ahs koh LAH ney) or *olive ripiene* (ree PYAY neh). The area around the town of Ancona produces huge green olives that are pitted, stuffed with a delicious combination of meats and Parmesan, then breaded and deep-fried—definitely labor-intensive! They are usually on the antipasto menu and well worth trying.

Pizza alla compagnola (PEET tsah ah lah kom pah NYOH lah). The traditional flatbread here in Le Marche is anointed with lard and topped with pork cracklings.

Quaglie in umido (KWAH lyeh een OO mee doh). This is quail, stewed in white wine and tomatoes and served over some type of starch, either polenta, risotto, or beans. Hunting for wild game in the hills of Le Marche is very popular, especially in the winter and spring months.

Sarde alla marchigiana (SAHR deh ah lah mar kee JAH nah). Sardines—fresh, not canned—are marinated with olive oil, rosemary, and parsley, then grilled or baked with bread crumbs.

Vincisgrassi (veen chee GRAH zee). This is a regional specialty, actually a type of lasagne, that dates back many centuries. The homemade noodles are baked with layers of different meats, tomatoes, mushrooms, black truffles, prosciutto, mozzarella, Parmesan, and béchamel sauce—just about everything that existed in the larder!

PIEMONTE (PIEDMONT)

Separated by the French Apennines on the northwest and Liguria and the Italian Riviera on the south, Piemonte, which translates as "foot of the mountain," is prone to hot summers, cold winters, and frequent thick fogs on its southern and eastern plains. Nevertheless, the Piemontesi are blessed with gentle hills and meadows that produce some of the world's finest foods and wines and a population with a love and understanding of their land and the patience to draw from it a *cucina* that is, in my opinion, unrivaled.

Autumn is the time when the *cucina* of Piemonte

approaches gastronomic paradise. That's when the intensely scented white truffles are ferreted out (in great secrecy) by specially bred hounds who help their masters uncover the valuable bounty. (Truffles are sold by weight, at over two hundred dollars per ounce!) Once dug up, the truffles begin to spoil and lose their intense perfume, so the fresher they are, the better. Enormous, fresh wild porcini appear in dishes from antipasto through *secondi*. Chestnuts and the world's best hazelnuts find their way into unforgettable desserts, delicious *torrone* (the nougat candy made here with hazelnuts, honey, and egg white) and *gianduja,* a mezmerizing marriage of hazelnuts and chocolate. The rich milk of sheep, goats, and cattle is used to make some of the most extraordinary cheeses in all of Italy, such as *castel-magno, tomino,* and *robiola.*

The wheaty-tasting, crunchy bread sticks known as *grissini* are so good that Napoleon is reported to have insisted on a daily delivery from Torino to Paris. The scope and quality of the antipasti are exceptional here in Piemonte and should not be missed. And then there are the wines! Deep red barolo and barbaresco are lauded worldwide, and the first-class barbera and dolcetto are ideal with the hearty local fare as well. A glass of the delicate dessert wine moscato, a type of sweet grape, is a must!

Bagna cauda (BAH nyah KAW dah). Literally, a "hot bath," this cold-weather appetizer from Piemonte is actually a dip comprised of hot olive oil flavored with garlic and anchovies into which raw vegetables such as celery, cardoons, fennel, and red and yellow peppers are dipped.

Bicerin (bee CHEH rin). This is a coffee specialty of Torino consisting of coffee, hot chocolate, and whipped cream.

Bollito misto (bol LEE toh MEES toh). Literally, a "mixture of boiled items," the lineup of which changes from region to region. In Piemonte, it generally consists of up to seven types of meat and poultry (perhaps beef, veal, tongue, chicken, goose, and pork sausage) accompanied by a piquant green sauce called *bagnet verde* (bahn YET VEYR deh), made with lots of parsley, olive oil, garlic, anchovies, lemon, bread crumbs, and a less pungent red sauce, *bagnet rosso* (ROS soh), containing tomatoes, red peppers, onion, garlic, and sweet basil. (See Menu Primer A to Z: *Bollito misto*.)

Bonet (bow NET). This is a delicious chocolate custard with ground amaretti (almond cookies) that's baked, then unmolded. The confectioners from Torino, the capital of Piemonte, are famous for their chocolate.

Brasato al barolo (bra SAHT oh al bar OH loh). This hearty, full-flavored dish features Piemonte's exceptional beef braised with another of its treasures—the wine barolo. A very special treat for the meat lover.

Capunet (kah poo NET). These are appetizers made of stuffed cabbage leaves (or, in summer, zucchini flowers) filled with assorted ground meats, eggs, garlic, herbs, and Parmesan, dipped in beaten egg and sautéed in butter.

Cisrà (CHEES rah). Chickpea soup, sometimes flavored with garlic, rosemary, and tomatoes, simmered in beef broth. Rice or pasta may be added as well.

Finanziera (fee nahn TSEE EH rah). This is a stew of chicken livers, sweetbreads, and other organ meats simmered with porcini and wine and named for the financial masters, who are reported to be especially fond of the dish.

Fonduta con tartufo (fon DOO tah kon tahr TOO foh). A signature dish of Piemonte (and also Valle d'Aosta), it's made in the fall, when white truffles are available. It's the Italian version of fondue, made from fontina, milk, egg yolks, and butter heated in the top of a double boiler until melted and smooth, then poured into a serving dish and topped with paper-thin slices of truffle. It's delicious all by itself, accompanied by vegetables, or over pasta.

Fritto misto (FREET toh MEES toh), or *Fricia* (FREE chah). In Piemonte, this daunting mixture of deep-fried foods will generally include lamb chops, sausage, chicken, organ meats such as sweetbreads and calves' liver, eggplant, zucchini, cubes of fried semolina (the hush puppies of Piemonte), and fruits such as peaches, pears, apples, and grapes, and—in case you're still hungry—almond cookies. (See Menu Primer A to Z: *Fritto misto*.)

Gianduja (jahn DOO yah). This delicious spread is made from chocolate and the excellent local hazelnuts. (See Menu Primer A to Z: *Crema*, Introduction above, and Market Buying Tips: *Cioccolato*.)

Gnocchi di patate (NYOH kee dee pah TAH teh). Potato dumplings are a specialty of this region and are sauced variously—with hearty meat sauces, the incredibly rich gorgonzola with butter and cream, or more simply with tomato sauce or melted butter with fried sage leaves.

Grissini (gree SEE nee). These are the fabulous bread sticks of Piemonte, stretching up to three feet long, served either wrapped in a napkin or just placed on the tablecloth. These handmade *grissini* are bumpy and uneven, light and crunchy. Legend has it that over three hundred years ago, the young Duke Vittorio Amadeo II of the House of Savoy had unremitting intestinal troubles and the court baker set out to bake the most digestible bread possible. He stretched his dough to such a degree that it consisted only of crust, and, happily, on a strict regimen of these tasty breadsticks, the duke was cured!

Insalata di carne cruda (een sah LAH tah dee KAHR neh KROO dah) or *carpaccio* (kahr PAH chyoh). A salad made from raw meat, usually lean veal, that is either sliced thin or ground and dressed with olive oil, lemon, salt, and pepper. In the fall, the salad can be topped with thin slices of white truffle—for a price, of course! Note: Although reports of illness due to contaminated raw meat have not been reported, those with compromised immune systems should always be aware of the possibility of contamination, and should avoid dishes like this.

Lepre in salmì (LAY pray een SAHL mee). This is wild hare that's marinated in red wine, vinegar, vegetables, and herbs, then browned and simmered in the red wine marinade.

Monte bianco (MON teh bee AHN koh). The Italian name for Mont Blanc, one of the highest peaks in Europe, after which this cone-shaped dessert is aptly named. It's made of pureed fresh chestnuts that are cooked with milk and vanilla, sweetened with sugar, then formed into a pyramid. This "mountain" is then frosted with whipped cream or meringue and chilled before serving.

Panissa (pah NEE sah). A regional version of risotto, the creamy, rich rice dish, this has sausage and beans.

Panna cotta (PAHN nah KOT tah). Literally, it translates as "cooked cream." On the menu, it's a rich, luscious custardlike dessert made with cooked-down cream, sugar, and gelatin (rather than eggs), with a caramelized sugar topping. Often served with pureed fruit or flavored with hazelnuts. A specialty of Piemonte.

Pasta

- *Agnolotti* (ahn nyoh LOH tee). These are small, usually meat-filled (but sometimes vegetable- or cheese-filled) pasta whose shapes can differ as widely as their fillings (half-moons, squares, or hats are just a few). Their sauces vary as well but often are as simple as butter with cream and *parmigiano-reggiano*.
- *Agnolotti del plin* (ahn nyoh LOH tee dehl PLEEN). In Alba, autumn brings this delicacy, in which the pasta is filled with a heavenly mixture of melted butter and white truffles.
- *Tajarin* (tah YAHR een). The thin, handmade egg noodles that are known as tagliarini elsewhere.

Pâté (pah TAY). Smooth, rich pâtés of chicken, pork, or wild fowl livers are very popular on the extensive antipasti platters of Piemonte.

Razza Piemontese (RAHT tzah). One of Italy's top cattle breeds, and beef is a popular meat in Piemonte.

Tartufi (tahr TOO fee). The white truffle of Piemonte, *Tuber magnatum*, is a fungus that grows a few inches beneath the ground under certain trees—oak, poplar, chestnut, and a few others. It's found from late September through January. During these months, paper-thin slices of truffle are shaved (with a special truffle-slicing tool) over carpaccio, in salads, or over hot bowls of pasta, risotto, and especially egg dishes. (See Market Buying Tips: *Tartufi*.)

Zabaione (zah bah YOH neh). This incredibly delicious dessert is made by whipping egg yolks with wine (usually marsala) and sugar and cooking the mixture over a flame until it has tripled in volume. Care must be taken in preparing the dish to prevent the egg yolks from scrambling. (See Menu Primer A to Z: *Zabaione*.)

PUGLIA (APULIA)

Like the other southern Mediterranean regions of Italy, Puglia is blessed with sunshine and dominated by the sea. But more than any other region in Italy, Puglia consists of flatlands. This paves the way for the production of an abundance of fine vegetables, which, in turn, play the largest role in the local *cucina*. A wide variety of greens are found, both cultivated and wild, as well as the eggplant and tomatoes that one would expect. Wheat is grown on the plains as well, and delicious breads and pastas (which are usually paired with whatever vegetables are in season) are important here. Both fruits and vegetables are preserved by drying them on wooden boards in the hot sun. Thick tomato paste is still made the old-fashioned way, by drying tomato sauce on these same wooden boards.

Fish and seafood predominate; mussels appear as part of the antipasti, in soups or with pasta, and snails—*lumache*—are not uncommon. Insist on having all of your seafood served cooked since raw seafood from local waters has been known to be contaminated. Meat is of lesser importance, except in the northernmost town of Foggia, where lamb dishes are featured. Veal, goat, and pork are also available. The *salumi* of Puglia, especially the ham *capocollo* and the sausage *cervellata*, both flavored with wine and pepper, are highly regarded.

Excellent cheeses, including the unusual *burrata*, which is filled with a soft, rich cream, are produced, especially inland. The aged ricotta, called *cacioricotta*, is sharply flavored and used for grating purposes. Olives are used in many dishes, and the olive oil is predominantly of the dense, richly flavored variety. Grape growing contributes in large part to the economy of Puglia, and the region produces over twenty DOC-designated wines.

Calzone (kahl TSOH nay). Pizza dough that is filled, often with fried onions, olives, tomatoes, anchovies, parsley, and pecorino or mozzarella, then folded over to make a half-moon shape and baked.

Cartellate o rose (kahr tel LAH teh oh RAWZ eh). These are rose-shaped pastries filled with a cooked mixture of jam, honey, and red wine. They are often served in restaurants after a meal and are delicious with coffee or wine.

Ciambotto (chee ahm BOHT toh). A sauce made from a variety of fish, it's used as a topping for pasta.

Ciceri e tria (chee CHER ee ay TREE ah). This is a hearty traditional dish in which chickpeas are served with strips of fried pasta.

Cozze fritte alla pugliese (KOH tsay FREET teh ah lah poo LYAY zay). Mussels that are dipped in flour, beaten egg, and bread crumbs, then fried. They're usually accompanied by lemon wedges.

Fave e cicoria (FAH vay ay chee KOHR yah). A classic dish of Puglia, it's made with pureed fava beans and chicory, a wild green native to the area, and flavored with the local pungent olive oil. The dish is also made with *lampasciuni* (lahm pahs CHOO nee), the small, bitter onions of the region.

Granita di caffè (grah NEE tah dee kah FAY). A delicious, dark, coffee-flavored slush. If you order a *speciale*, it will be topped with whipped cream.

Lumache all'origano (loo MAH keh ahl oh ree GHAN noh). Snails, cooked Pugliese-style, using the wild oregano that grows in the region. They're prepared with oregano, mint, salt, pepper, garlic, and olive oil.

Maritata (mahr ee TAH tah). A soup in which several vegetables, usually fennel, chicory, escarole, and celery, are boiled together to "marry" the flavors, then layered with pecorino and pepper and covered with broth.

Pane (PAH nay). The native bread of the region, *pane pugliese* (PAH nay poo LYAY zay), is highly revered for its rustic, chewy texture, a result of the less-refined flours used to make these huge round loaves. The delicious *puccia* (poo CHEE ah) loaf is studded with salty black olives.

Panzarotti (pahn tsah ROHT tee). These are fried breads stuffed with any number of fillings, from vegetables to meats or cheeses.

Pasta

- *Laganelle* (lah ghan EL leh). Lasagnalike sheets of pasta.
- *Orecchiette* (oh rek KYET teh). This pasta, shaped like little ears, is most popular in Puglia. When served *con cime di rapa* (kon CHEE meh dee RAH pah), it's topped with turnip greens that have been sautéed with garlic, hot chili peppers, and often anchovies. Other vegetables such as broccoli—*cime di broccoletti* (CHEE meh dee brawk koh LEHT tee), cauliflower—*cavolfiore* (kah vol FYO reh), eggplant—*melanzana* (mey lahn TSAH nah), or chicory—*cicoria* (chee KOHR yah) may be used. The "little ears" of pasta traditionally

have been made—by hand—mostly of semolina, plus a little plain flour and water. They're made on wooden boards—often outdoors, so the cook can enjoy the sunshine. The little hollows in the pasta are perfect for capturing bits of sauce. In some areas, they are called *strascinati* (strah shee NAH tee), which means "dragged" (pushed with the thumb or finger against the board), the method for creating the shape. When the cook has dragged a little too enthusiastically, the pasta closes more, and they become known in the local dialect as *cavatiedde* (kahv ah TYAYD deh), a.k.a. *cavatelli*.

Tiella or *teglia* (TYAYL lah or TEH lyah). Literally, the term for a "casserole dish." The casserole can be made of a variety of vegetables, such as broccoli and cauliflower, rice, mussels, potatoes, and perhaps pecorino cheese.

Triglia di scoglio (TREE lyah dee SKOH lyoh). This is red mullet, a popular menu item in Puglia, served grilled. The sauce becomes colored by the fish's red skin.

SARDEGNA (SARDINIA)

As an isolated island in the Mediterranean, Sardegna has historically been a closed world, with few external forces shaping its culture or *cucina*. It did, however, spend several centuries under Spain's rule. In particular, the Catalans settled in Alghero, and remnants of their language, culture, and food remain today. Until 1950, most Sardinians lived inland because the marshy coastline was plagued by malaria. The inhospitable mountainous terrain furthered their isolation and provided a meager living for the people. Sardinians have only become oriented to the sea in the last fifty years. Once the marshlands were drained and made habitable, however, the natives were able to take advantage of the seacoast, its beaches, and the bounty of the sea.

Sheepherding was the major occupation over the centuries, and the by-products of cheese—especially pecorino—milk, and meat dominate the cuisine. Sardinian sheep's milk cheese, *pecorino sardo,* is prized throughout Italy, but samples differ widely depending on the source and the age of the cheese, from soft and mild to hard and tangy. Ewe's-milk ricotta is outstanding as well. Fishing has become a common occupation, and the local lobsters called *aragoste,* and other seafood are now found on most menus.

Wild herbs such as mint, fennel, bay leaves, rosemary, and the abundantly available leaves of the myrtle tree are the island's seasonings. Sardegna produces delicious honeys, both sweet and bitter, which are used in most of the regional pastries, many of which are made with almonds.

Agnello al finocchio (ahn YEL loh ahl fee NOHK yoh). Lamb with fennel features two of Sardegna's major tastes. Chunks of lamb are browned in olive oil, then cooked with onion, tomatoes, and the licorice-tasting fennel.

Aragosta (ahr ah GOSE tah). Spiny clawless lobster. (See Menu Primer A to Z: *Aragosta*.)

Arselle (ahr SEHL leh). These are delicately flavored, wedge-shaped clams common to the region.

Bottarga (bot TAR gah). Mullet roe or eggs, dried and pressed. It's used to flavor salads and bean dishes. (See Menu Primer A to Z: *Bottarga*.)

Carta da musica (KAHR tah dah MOO zee kah) or *pane carasau* (PAH nay kah rah SAH oo). This thin, crisp crackerlike bread was the staff of life for shepherds who were tending their flocks. It had great keeping qualities and provided sustenance on protracted travels, along with some pecorino (sheep's cheese) and wine.

Cassola (kahs SOH lah). This is the local fish stew, with Catalan influences, that contains twelve varieties of fish, crab, and chili peppers.

Fregula (FRAY goo lah) "Crumbs," hand-formed from semolina, water, and saffron, are made both small and large; the smaller version is added to soups, usually chicken broth, while the larger one is used as pasta, usually topped with tomato sauce.

Malloreddus (mahl loh RED doos). These Sardinian gnocchi (NYOH kee) are made with semolina and the locally grown saffron; they're sauced in various ways but invariably topped with the tangy Sardinian pecorino.

Minestra con i finocchi (mee NES trah kon ee fee NOK kee). Fennel soup, a natural result of the abundance of fennel that grows on the island. The chopped fennel is cooked in olive oil, simmered in broth, and seasoned simply with parsley or wild herbs.

Mirto (MEER toh). Myrtle is a common flavoring in the food of Sardegna, but the name also refers to the after-dinner liqueur made from the myrtle tree.

Pane frattau (PAH nay frah TAH oo). A classic dish of the region in which the thin cracker-type bread *pane carasau* (PAH nay kah rah SAH oo) is briefly soaked in hot water, then layered with tomato sauce, pecorino, and a fried egg.

Pasta

• *Impanadas* (eem pah NAH das). These are meat-filled pasta that are oven baked. As the name suggests, the influence is Spanish.

Pastu mistu (pahs TOO MEES too). This remarkable dish consists of an enormous turkey whose cavity is stuffed with a whole duck, a chicken, a partridge, and perhaps a lark, then cooked in a large pit lined with branches of myrtle.

Polpette d'agnello (pohl PET teh d'ahn YEL loh). Here in Sardegna, ground lamb is made into delicious meatballs and seasoned with wild herbs, often mint.

Porceddu (por CHED doo). This is the most famous of all Sardinian dishes. It's milk-fed pig, seasoned with fresh herbs and myrtle leaves and spit-roasted over an open fire.

Seadas (sey AH dahs). These fried, cheese-filled pastries topped with honey are found throughout Sardegna.

SICILIA (SICILY)

Sicily, the largest island in the Mediterranean, is situated west of the toe of the Italian boot, separated from the mainland by the Ionian Sea. Unlike Sardegna, which remained largely isolated throughout most of its history, Sicily managed to play host to an inordinate number of alien rulers, from the Greeks to the Saracens, Arabs, Normans, Spanish, and Italians—to name just a few! Their legacy remains today in the kitchens of Sicily, where tastes of these cultures (such as *agrodolce*, or the sweet-sour combination of the Saracens) still reverberate.

Although much of the island is sun-parched and rainfall is slight, agricultural products such as wheat, citrus fruits, olives, vegetables (especially eggplant, tomatoes, and artichokes), almonds, pistachios, and capers are of ethereal quality. Seafood is much preferred to meat; tuna, swordfish, sardines, and anchovies play starring roles in the Sicilian *cucina*, along with octopus, clams, squid, mussels, and many more curious kinds of seafood. Sicilian cuisine is a remarkable combination of *cucina povera*, the food of the poor (who nevertheless enjoy first-class raw ingredients), and extremely complex dishes required by the various members of the nobility throughout the centuries. Vineyards are plentiful, but most of the grapes are made into one of the world's most popular dessert wines, marsala, which appears in both sweet and savory dishes here in Sicily, throughout Italy, and beyond. The luscious dessert zabaione and veal marsala are two such examples. (See Market Buying Tips: *Marsala*.)

Desserts reach celestial heights here in Sicilia in answer to the characteristic sweet tooth handed down from the Saracens, who grew sugarcane. Traditionally, sweets were more than indulgence—they played significant, ritualistic roles in religion, which was heavily laced with superstition. Cannoli, the delicious cylinders of sweet pastry filled with ricotta, sugar, and candied fruit, were fertility symbols, served primarily at weddings and later associated with Easter. Many of the sweets were made in monasteries and convents and had mystical connotations. Marzipan, or almond paste, which appears in many of the confections, is thought to be of Saracen origins as well. The credit for Italy's sublime answer to ice cream, *gelato*, also goes to the Arabs.

Cannoli (kah NOH lee). Sweet ricotta-filled pastry tubes. (See above and Menu Primer A to Z: *Cannoli*.)

Caponata (kah poh NAH tah). An age-old Sicilian eggplant dish whose sweet and sour *(agrodolce)* notes show the influence of the Saracen invasion. A wonderful vegetable dish with layers of flavor, it's made with a variable list of vegetables (each cooked separately), but it always has eggplant and usually celery, onion, tomatoes, zucchini, raisins, olives, capers, pine nuts, vinegar, and sugar. The "sweet" note is from raisins and sugar, the "sour" from wine vinegar. Served hot or at room temperature, it can appear as an appetizer, an accompaniment to meat, or even a pasta sauce. The best comes from the city of Palermo.

Cassata siciliana (kah SAH tah see cheel YAH nah). This classic dessert is an Easter specialty. Its base is sponge cake filled variously with a sweet wine-spiked ricotta, custard, or ice cream and dotted with candied fruit, pistachio nuts, and bits of chocolate. A layer of almond paste (marzipan) often encases the cake. (See Menu Primer A to Z: *Cassata*.)

Cavolfiore (kah vol FYO reh). Cauliflower of exceptional quality are grown in Sicily. Of special note is the purple variety, often served in omelettes called *frittate* (freet TAH tay).

Cuscus (KOOS koos). This is the Sicilian word for "couscous," which frequently appears as a first course, once again reflecting the residual North African influence.

Panelle (pah NEHL leh). These are delicious deep-fried fritters made from chickpea flour that are commonly sold on street corners in Sicily.

Pasta alla Norma (PAH stah ah lah NOR mah). A well-known pasta dish created in honor of the first performance of *Norma*, the most famous opera by Sicily's favorite son Vincenzo Bellini. It's comprised of the typical ingredients of the region—tomatoes, onion, garlic, and fried eggplant.

Pasta con le sarde (PAH stah kon lay SAHR deh). Echoes of the sweet-sour legacy of North African conquerors are at play in this distinctly Sicilian pasta dish. Most representative of the city of Palermo, it consists of fennel, onions, raisins or currants, pine nuts, and saffron sautéed in olive oil, then layered with spaghetti and fresh sardines and baked in the oven.

Pasta reale (PAH stah reh AH leh). Not a pasta in the usual sense, this is the highly acclaimed almond paste, or marzipan, of Sicilia. It's used in countless dessert preparations.

Pesce spada (PAY shay SPAH dah). Swordfish. (See Menu Primer A to Z: *Pesce spada*.)

Sarde a beccafico (SAHR deh ah bek kah FEE koh). These are sardines stuffed with a mixture of raisins and pine nuts, bread crumbs, garlic, pepper, and olive oil, then dusted with flour and fried.

Sfinciuni (sfeen CHYOO nee). These are Palermo's bready pizzas with soft, puffy dough and toppings such as the local ricotta or caciocavallo, tomato sauce, oregano, and perhaps a little sausage, salami, or anchovy.

Tonno (TOHN noh). Fresh tuna is caught in May or June (depending on the weather and other mysterious conditions) along Sicilia's western coastline. Excitement rises as the carefully orchestrated ancient ritual takes place. Many-chambered nets entrap the tuna, and fishermen encircle and spear the prized catch. Several different preparations are found, and many employ such other trademark tastes of the island as capers. This dish is called *tonno ai capperi* (kahp PEH ree); tuna steaks are marinated in wine, garlic, and herbs such as rosemary, then grilled and sauced with olive oil, lemon juice, and capers. (See Menu Primer A to Z: *Tonno*.)

Zabaione (zah bah YON eh), or *zabaglione*. (See Menu Primer A to Z: *Zabaione*.)

TOSCANA (TUSCANY)

The magnificent landscape of Toscana is etched in the minds of all who have admired the works of Michelangelo and Leonardo da Vinci, for it is Tuscany where these and other Renaissance artists often lived and its world that they depicted. Toscana is nestled in Italy's heartland, and Firenze was at the heart of the Renaissance, truly the rebirth of the Italian spirit. The Renaissance dominated the region in all facets of culture with its predisposition for restraint, harmony, and balance in all things. This inherent discipline spilled over into the *cucina*, in which quality and simplicity are revered and gluttony and excess frowned upon.

And so it seems right that the cornerstones of Tuscan cuisine are exquisite but humble—bread (made without salt) and olive oil—and their presence is invoked in countless Tuscan specialties. All cultures seek to make use of their stale bread, but in Toscana, this has been raised to an art form. Delicious soups such as *ribollita* and *pappa col pomodoro* were created to recycle the bread, which serves to thicken and stretch the dish. They are, of course, enriched with a generous sprinkling of the fragrant and peppery green-tinged olive oil.

This is the region where *bistecca alla fiorentina*—grilled T-bone steak, Florentine-style—reigns. But even this extravagance, from the prized breed known as Chianina (kee ah NEE nah), is treated with restraint—charcoal-grilled, rubbed with garlic and sea salt, and drizzled with Tuscan olive oil. White beans, almost always *cannellini*, are synonymous with the region and are cooked with varying ingredients but invariably—you guessed it—with olive oil. Vegetables are plentiful and generally simply prepared—and dressed with olive oil. The association of Florence with spinach may be somewhat exaggerated in the rest of the world, however, for the term "Florentine" does not always suggest its presence.

The region has produced wine since Etruscan times; this is the land of traditional reds such as chianti and brunello di Montalcino. Much innovation and experimentation is taking place today in wine making in Toscana, and the subject deserves investigation!

Acquacotta (AHK wah KOHT tah). This thin vegetable soup (the literal translation is "cooked water") can range from simple to elaborate. It's served over a toasted slice of stale bread, enriched with olive oil and often topped with a poached egg.

Anguilla alla fiorentina (ahn GWEEL lah ah lah fyor ehn TEE nah). This is eel, Florentine-style. The eels are first browned in olive oil, then baked with garlic, wine, fresh herbs, and, of course, olive oil. (See Menu Primer A to Z: *Anguilla*.)

Arista (ah REES tah). Roast pork loin. (See Menu Primer A to Z: *Arista*.)

Baccalà alla livornese (bah kah LAH ah lah lee vor NAY zay). From the town of Livorno comes this version of the dried, salt-cured cod. It's braised with lemon, garlic, parsley, and white wine and often includes slices of cooked tripe. (See Menu Primer A to Z: *Baccalà*.)

Biscottini di Prato (bees kot TEE nee dee PRAH toh). These are dry almond cookies that are always served after meals with *vin santo*, the sweet dessert wine. Although *biscotti* are found throughout the country, this small industrial town north of Firenze is reputed to make the finest—perfect for pairing with Toscana's excellent *vin santo*.

Bistecca alla fiorentina (bees TEK kah al lah fyor en TEE nah). This classic Florentine dish typifies Toscana as no other dish can. It's made with the revered Chianina (kee ah NEE nah) beef, one of Italy's two most prized breeds of cattle. (The other is Piemonte's *razza piemontese*.) The beef is seasoned with crushed black peppercorns, cooked just until rare over a wood-burning or charcoal fire, then rubbed with garlic and sea salt and drizzled with Tuscan olive oil. This is the ultimate to beef-loving Italians.

Cacciucco (kaht CHOO koh). Fish soup. (See Menu Primer A to Z: *Cacciucco*.)

Crostini al fegato (krohs TEE nee ahl feh GAH toh). Thin slices of Tuscan bread, toasted, then anointed with a warm topping of finely minced or pureed chicken livers. They are encountered on any Tuscan antipasto worth its salt. *Crostini di milza* (MEEL tsah) are topped with minced spleen.

Fagioli (fah JOH lee). Beans. In Tuscany this usually means the white *cannellini* (kahn nel LEEN nee), which are similar to our great northern beans. (Excellent green beans are also served in Toscana.) When listed as *al fiasco* (fee AHS koh), they are prepared in traditional fashion. First they are placed in a large glass chianti flask with water, garlic, and olive oil, and sage leaves are wedged into the flask's neck to seal in the vapors. The flask is set in the smoldering embers of a brick oven and left to cook. The tender cooked beans are mixed with lemon juice, salt, pepper, and more olive oil. *Insalata di fagioli al tonno* (een sah LAH tah . . . ahl TOHN noh) is a salad of *cannellini* with tuna, lemon juice, onion, salt, and pepper. *Fagioli all'uccelletto* (oot chel LEHT toh) is a popular winter dish in which the white beans are cooked with tomatoes, garlic, and fresh sage leaves and served with spiced sausages.

Fettunta (fet TOON tah). This is the Tuscan name for *bruschetta*, thick slices of rustic Tuscan bread, toasted, rubbed with garlic, and drizzled with (naturally!) Tuscan extra virgin olive oil.

Finocchiona (feen nok KYOH nah). Tuscan fennel-flavored pork sausage.

Fiori di zucca fritti (FYO ree dee TSOOK kah FREET tee). These are zucchini blossoms, usually stuffed with mozzarella, then battered and deep-fried.

Fritto misto alla fiorentina (FREET toh MEES toh ah lah fyor en TEE nah). In Florence, the "mixed fry" consists of battered and deep-fried pieces of chicken, rabbit, and sometimes lamb chops, along with vegetables such as artichokes, zucchini and zucchini flowers, and mushrooms. It is served garnished with lemon wedges and often accompanied by polenta.

Panzanella (pahn zah NEL lah). Tuscan bread salad of tomatoes, cucumbers, onion, and fresh basil combined with cubes of stale bread moistened with olive oil. The frugal Tuscan housewives made many such dishes using leftover bread. Traditionally they made these dishes for lack of money; now they make them because they taste good. (See Menu Primer A to Z: *Panzanella*.)

Pappa col pomodoro (PAHP pah kol pom oh DAW roh). Tuscan tomato soup thickened with stale bread, flavored with garlic and basil, and enriched with olive oil. (See Menu Primer A to Z: *Minestra* and *Pappa col pomodoro*.)

Pappardelle (pahp pahr DEHL lay). A favorite form of pasta in this region is the homemade wide noodle with curly edges called *pappardelle*. It's perfect served with wild game sauces, such as those made with wild hare—*alla lepre* (LAY pray). The rich, meaty sauce is made with onion, garlic, celery, tomato paste, and red wine and flavored with juniper berries and rosemary.

Pasta e fagioli (PAH stah ay fah JOH lee). This is a hearty soup made with pasta and dried beans that appears throughout Italy and beyond. (See Menu Primer A to Z: *Pasta e fagioli*.)

Pici (PEE chee). Delicious, toothsome, hand-rolled spaghetti found in Toscana, often sauced simply with lots of garlic and extra virgin olive oil and parsley.

Pinzimonio (peen tzee MOHN yoh). When the peppery green oil of the region is newly pressed, fresh vegetables such as endive, carrots, fennel, and celery are dipped in the oil to which only salt and pepper have been added. This is a dish that emphasizes the reverence Tuscans feel toward their oil.

Piselli al prosciutto (pee SEL lee ahl pro SHOOT toh). In springtime, when tiny, new peas appear in the markets, it's time for this simple dish in which peas are cooked with onion and prosciutto and sautéed in olive oil.

Prosciutto di cinghiale (pro SHOOT toh dee cheen GYAH lay). The wild boar of Toscana is made into delicious salt- and air-cured ham. It's a frequent member of the antipasto platter.

Ravioli (rah VYOH lee). Here in Toscana they are likely to be filled with ricotta and chopped spinach.

Ribollita (ree bohl LEE tah). Literally, "reboiled." This is a hearty Tuscan soup thickened with bread. (See Menu Primer A to Z: *Minestra* and *Ribollita*.)

Schiacciata al rosmarino (skyaht CHYAH tah ahl rawz mah REE noh). This Tuscan flatbread is sprinkled with coarse salt and topped with olive oil and fresh herbs, usually rosemary or sage. *Schiacciata con l'uva* is a dessert bread that dates back to Etruscan times. It's topped with grapes and sugar in celebration of the grape harvest.

Trippa alla fiorentina (TREEP pah ah lah fyor en TEE nah). Tripe, the stomach of such ruminants as cows and sheep, is highly favored in Toscana, where it's cooked with tomatoes and topped with Parmesan.

TRENTINO–ALTO ADIGE

In the mountainous northeast portion of Italy lie the hyphenated regions of Trentino, to the south, and Alto Adige, to the north. Although these two regions are linked by geography and traditions, there are differences in their culture, language, and, to some extent, their food. Trentino's spirit is Italian, with strong ties to Veneto, and, to a lesser extent, to the Germanic nations to the north. Alto Adige is a German-speaking region, which up until World War I was part of the Austrian empire, and the preponderance of cultural influences are from Austria and Germany.

The *cucina* is substantial, filling fare, and meats, wild game, goulash, soups, and starches are major contributors. Pasta takes a backseat to the other starches in the region, however. Traditionally, polenta (Veneto's influence) was served as the main starch, especially in Trentino, and it remains on menus today, usually as a side dish for meats or sausages. Some polenta is made from buckwheat instead of corn. Apples are grown in the valleys of Alto Adige and appear most often in desserts (especially in strudel) throughout both regions. In Trentino, a wide variety of mushrooms grow in abundance, and from Lake Garda come lovely trout, *trota*, a lighter choice for dinner amid all the meat and game. Excellent cow's milk cheeses, such as Malga are produced, but many of the names change from town to town, making it difficult to recommend any in particular. Look for the word *nostrano*, which means "ours," implying the cheese is homemade.

Canederli (kahn AY dayr lee). These are dumplings made of bread, either white or rye. Often they receive a flavor boost from a variety of additions, including liver, ham, cheese, herbs, especially parsley, and spices, often nutmeg. They can be served in broth or as a side dish for meats. *Canederli* are a heavier dumpling than the gnocchi of other regions, but they are highly appropriate for the colder northern climate.

Capriolo (kahp ree OH loh). This is roebuck, which is often cooked in a red currant sauce, *al ribes* (ahl REE behs). Many of the game dishes served in the region are accompanied by sweet fruit sauces.

Crauti (KRAH oo tee). Sauerkraut is found on most menus in the region, and it is often flavored with juniper berries, cooked with pork fat, and served as the accompaniment to meat. *Sauerkraut suppe* (sah oor krah OOT SOOP peh), soup made with sauerkraut, is reputed to return the digestive tract to health following alcoholic overindulgence.

Minestra d'orzo (mee NES trah D'OR zoh). Barley soup, to which white beans are often added, uses either water or broth as its base. The soup is flavored with onion, bacon, carrot, celery, and tomatoes. (See Menu Primer A to Z: *Minestra d'orzo.*)

Pasta

- *Schlutz krapfen* (SCHLUTZ krap fen). These are large ravioli that come with various fillings, often potatoes with herbs, cheese, or even sauerkraut.
- *Tirtlen* (TERT len). Pasta filled with cheese or vegetables, then fried.

Smacafam (SMAH kah fahm). The literal translation is "hunger-killer," and this polenta and sausage combo is guaranteed to deliver!

Speck (SPEK). This is the traditional brine-cured bacon of the region, salted and peppered, then slow-smoked. In the past, the process took several months, but today artisans who follow the old ways are hard to find. Most of the *Speck* available today is industrially made, and smoking takes place in weeks rather than months.

Strudel (STROO dehl). The Austrian sweet tooth has remained intact here, and strudel, filled mainly with apples but also with pears or occasionally cherries, is available everywhere.

Tortell di patate (tor TEHL dee pah TAH teh). These crispy potato pancakes, a reflection of the German influence, are often served as part of the antipasto along with the ubiquitous cured pork products.

UMBRIA

One of the few regions of Italy without a coastline, Umbria is known for its quiet medieval hilltop towns, the hearty simplicity of its food, and for its beautiful majolica pottery produced in the town of Deruta. Despite its proximity to both Toscana and Lazio, Umbria retains a serene quality, with the exception of its capital, Perugia, which has become more cosmopolitan over the last decade or two. (Buitoni pasta is produced here as is Perugina chocolate.)

Although landlocked, the region nevertheless boasts lakes and rivers teeming with eel, freshwater shrimp, and fish. The arable land is limited, but fertile, and since antiquity has produced emmer, or *farro*, a grain credited with sustaining the ancient Roman legions. Today Umbria produces more wheat than emmer, but the rich, nutty-tasting grain still appears on the table. First-class lentils, *lenticchie*, are also grown here. Olive trees thrive, even on rocky hillsides, and the olive oil is plentiful and of prime quality.

The cooking of Umbria is simple and straight-forward; little headway has been made here by trendy upstarts. Each ingredient (there are usually no more than three or four per dish) stands up to be counted. Umbrian olive oil is spectacular, full-flavored and fragrant, and it's the condiment of choice for topping soups, *bruschetta*, fish—almost anything. Both veal and lamb as well as wild game play prominent roles on the menu, almost always prepared simply by roasting or grilling.

Anguilla alla brace (ahn GWEEL lah ah lah BRAH chay). Eel from Lago di Trasimeno are considered a great delicacy, and in this preparation they are simply grilled.

Bruschetta (broos KET tah). Thick slices of bread, toasted, rubbed with garlic, and drizzled with olive oil. In Umbria, other adornments such as black truffles or fava beans may also appear on the bread.

Capocollo (kah poh KOHL loh). One of the most common of the cured pork *salumi* on the antipasto menu. In Umbria, a specially cured *salame* is prepared for Easter, when it is eaten along with cheese-topped focaccia and hard-boiled eggs as an appetizer and drunk with white wine.

Crostini (krohs TEE nee). Thin slices (as opposed to the thicker slices of *bruschetta*) of coarse-textured bread, toasted, with various toppings such as the delicous black Umbrian olives or fresh porcini. Served as an antipasto.

Fagiano all'uva (fah GYAH noh ahl OO vah). Wild pheasant cooked with grapes.

Frittata di tartufi (freet TAH tah dee tahr TOO fee). This is an omelette made with black truffles. The addition of a few waferlike slices of truffle elevates the frittata to new heights.

Lepre alle olive (LAY pray ah lay oh LEE vay). This is a popular regional dish in which wild hare is cooked with olives, fresh herbs, and wine.

Minestra di farro (mee NES trah dee FAR roh). Umbria's arable land is limited, but fertile, and since antiquity has produced emmer, or *farro*, a grain credited with sustaining the ancient Roman legions. Today Umbria produces more wheat than emmer, but the rich, nutty-tasting grain still appears on the table in wonderful, sturdy soups, with tomatoes and other vegetables and flavored with a prosciutto bone. (See Market Buying Tips: *Farro.*)

Palombe or *palombacci* (pah LOM beh or pah lom BAH chee). This is spit-roasted wood pigeon. In Umbria, spit roasting, grilling, and baking in wood-burning ovens are the cooking methods of choice for both wild game and domestic meats, and each procedure imparts a distinctive flavor to the simple preparations. Pigeon is usually served with a sauce called *la ghiotta* (GYOHT tah), which is made by combining the juices thrown off by the cooking process combined with olives, olive oil, vinegar, anchovies, lemon, and wild sage leaves.

Pasta

- *Spaghetti alla Norcina* (spah GET tee ah lah nor CHEE nah). This dish may feature the local black truffles in an olive oil–based sauce spiked with garlic and anchovies. But just to confuse matters, the same name is given to a spaghetti dish made with sausage (*salsiccia*) (from the renowned sausage makers of Norcia) and cream.
- *Stringozzi* (streen GOHT tsee), *manfrigoli* (mahn free GOH lee), and *umbricelli* (oom bree CHEL lee). The wheaty taste of emmer, or *farro*, in this thick, sturdy handmade pasta is immediately apparent. These rustic pastas are generally dressed with tomato and garlic.

Pollo in porchetta. (See Menu Primer A to Z: *Pollo: Porchetta.*)

Porchetta (por KET tah). Suckling pig baked in a wood-burning oven and seasoned with garlic, rosemary, wild fennel, and mint. Chicken and fish such as carp are accorded the same delectable preparation.

Prosciutto di cinghiale (pro SHOOT toh dee cheen GHEE ah leh). The famous pork butchers of Norcia make a very special prosciutto from wild boar. It's saltier than the prosciutto of Parma but well suited to the unsalted bread of Umbria. It's often served at the beginning of the meal as part of the antipasto.

Regina in porchetta (ray GEE nah een por KET tah). Carp from Umbria's Lago di Trasimeno are featured in a dish called *regina in porchetta*. Although the term *porchetta* would lead you to believe this is a pork dish, it is not. In this preparation, the fish are seasoned with garlic, rosemary, wild fennel, and mint and baked in a wood-burning oven in the same manner as the *porchetta*, the small suckling pig.

Rocciate (roh CHYAH teh). A delicious filling of fruit and nuts is rolled in a sweet dough to form cylinders. It's wonderful with a glass of sweet wine!

Salsiccia di cinghiale (sahl SEET chah dee cheen GHEE ah leh). Wild boar sausage. Umbrian pork butchers, especially those from the town of Norcia, are renowned for their wild boar sausages, which are often served *con lenticchie* (len TEE kee ay), with lentils.

Schiacciata (skyaht CHYAH tah). Flatbread. Here in Umbria, flatbreads are still baked on open wood-fueled hearths. They are topped simply, with vegetables, perhaps onion, and good fruity olive oil. They make a great snack or appetizer.

Tegamaccio (tey gah MAH chyoh). This is Umbria's version of fish stew. Because the region is landlocked, the fish used are obviously freshwater and include trout, carp, and pike.

VALLE D'AOSTA

Surrounded by Switzerland, France, and the Piemonte region, Valle d'Aosta, the smallest and least-populated region of Italy, is dominated by its spectacular mountains, including the famous snow-capped Monte Bianco. Castles and mountain hamlets provide a picturesque backdrop for today's visitors, who come to admire the scenery, visit the beautiful Gran Paradiso National Park, or ski. Valle d'Aosta is a bilingual region where French and Italian are spoken and the two cultures coexist.

Throughout the centuries, the forests yielded magnificent game, especially chamois, *camoscio,* and ibex, venison, wild hare, and boar. Alpine meadows provided grass for grazing cattle. Consequently, the *cucina* featured rich game dishes, beef, kid *(capretto)*, and veal, and they remain on menus today, often stewed with red wine or grappa. Wonderfully rich dairy products, including cheeses (especially the deservedly famous, delicately flavored fontina), milk, and butter contribute much to the local cuisine.

Throughout the centuries, the stockpot simmered continuously on the back of the stove, and the resulting soups sustained the population on cold winter nights. Rustic country bread was another element basic to Aosta cooking. Called *pane nero,* or "black bread," it's still made with some combination of rye, barley, and hard wheat flour. Rice and polenta take the place of pasta dishes. Excellent apples, pears, and honey are produced here, and they frequently appear in dishes on the dessert menu.

Boudin (boo DEEN). This is blood sausage or "pudding" made with potatoes, beets, and spices. It appears on the antipasto platter, but it's also served with potatoes as a main course.

Caffè alla Valdostana (kah FAY ah lah vahl dos TAH nah). A delicious after-dinner coffee tradition particular to the region, this "cup of friendship" consists of coffee, lemon peel, grappa, and sugar and is served in a multispouted communal cup that is shared by all at the table.

Carbonada (kahr boh NAH dah). This is a very old dish consisting of salted beefsteak, smoked bacon, garlic, and wine and seasoned with cinnamon, cloves, and pepper. The meat is slow-cooked and served with firm polenta.

Cotoletta alla valdostana (kot oh LET tah ah lah vahl dos TAH nah). This is a veal chop, or cutlet, cut horizontally and stuffed with a slice of fontina. The chop is seasoned, dipped in beaten egg, then in bread crumbs, and cooked in butter. Sometimes it's adorned with a slice of prosciutto and thinly sliced white truffles.

Fonduta (fon DOO tah). Fondue, the famous dish of melted cheese used for dipping cubes of bread, is exceptional in Valle d'Aosta, because it's made with the region's fabulous fontina. (See Regional/Seasonal Specialties: Piemonte: *Fonduta con tartufo* and Market Buying Tips: *Formaggi: Fontina.*)

Gnocchi alla valdostana (NYOH kee ah lah vahl dos TAH nah). The region's wonderful potato and flour dumplings are topped with creamy fontina (fon TEE nah).

Mocetta (maw CHET tah). Traditionally, this was the leg of chamois, mountain goat, or ibex, cured like prosciutto. Today this specialty is often made with beef.

Polenta concia (poh LEHN tah kon chah). This is the cornmeal mush that is found throughout the northern regions. In Valle d'Aosta, it's made rich and delicious with fontina and butter.

Seupetta di cogne (tsoo PEHT tah dee KOH nyeh). This hearty soup is made of broth, rice, butter, and fontina and thickened with stale, dark bread.

Seuppa or *zuppa alla valdostana* (TSOOP pah ah lah vahl dos TAH nah). This "soup" is based on the region's ubiquitous homemade meat stock. It consists of layers—first dark bread is placed on the bottom of an ovenproof dish. Green cabbage is placed on top of the bread, along with fontina, butter, and finally, the stock, and then baked in the oven for thirty to forty minutes, after which the name "soup" hardly applies.

Zuppa do castagne (TSOOP pah doh kas TAN nyay). This soup, made of chestnuts, rice, and milk, is especially popular in autumn, when the chestnuts fall.

VENETO

Located in the northeastern part of Italy, Veneto has a varied landscape, from the coastal lagoons on the Adriatic Sea to the foothills of the Alps, with fertile plains in between. The topography has created diverse climates and conditions, and each area produces its own specialties, from seafood to meats, rice, corn, and vegetables.

Venice, or Venezia, with its easy access to the sea, was famous throughout history for its domination of the lucrative spice trade. Venetians became both expert navigators and merchants, and Italy became a huge market for the flavors of the Eastern civilizations. Pepper, saffron (from the Arabs), cinnamon, mace, and cloves, as well as exotic fruits such as raisins and oranges, were imported. Yet most Venetians were hardworking, simple people who preferred simple foods. These two sides of the Venetian character were displayed in the cuisine, resulting in dishes that, though humble, were often refined to a previously unknown degree.

Few Americans will recognize much of the local bounty of the sea, but the freshness of the seafood and the simplicity of its preparation can generally be expected. Meat, poultry, and game appear more on menus inland, but the famous local calves' liver and onions, *fegato alla veneziana,* is easily found. Rice and corn grow readily in the region. Risotto, made from *vialone nano,* the particular short-grained rice grown here, is used in a dizzying number of first-course dishes that display the extraordinary imagination of the local cooks. And polenta, made from the fine-ground cornmeal that sustained the masses for centuries, still plays a huge role on today's menus. Excellent vegetables appear in the markets and on menus—sweet young peas and asparagus in the springtime and the finest radicchio in the fall months. The cheese asiago of Veneto is excellent and may be found young and creamy or aged and quite pungent. Venetians have a sweet tooth, and tiramisù is ubiquitous. Other desserts can recall Veneto's adventurous past when they contain raisins, pine nuts, almonds, and spices.

Anatra (or *anitra*) *col pien* (AH nah tra kol pee EHN). "Duck with stuffing," a signature dish of Veneto, can be boiled, roasted, or stuffed, perhaps with liver, veal, and bacon made into a paste with bread crumbs, Parmesan, and herbs. In Italy, ducks are somewhat leaner than those in America.

Anguilla alla spiedo (ahn GWEEL lah ah lah SPYEY doh). This is eel, cubed and spit-roasted with cubes of bread and bay leaves.

Baccalà (bah kah LAH). This is dried, salt-cured cod that's used in many Venetian dishes, including *mantecato* (mahn teh KAH toh), a delicious and unusual first course in the region. (See Menu Primer A to Z: *Baccalà: Mantecato* and *Vincentina*.)

Bellini (bel LEE nee). A famous cocktail created at the famous Harry's Bar in Venezia, made with Prosecco, a sparkling white wine, and peach puree. (See Beverages A to Z: *Bellini*.)

Bigoli (bee GO lee). This is a hearty, handmade spaghetti made with a spaghetti press called a *torchio*. A signature dish of Veneto, it's often served *in salsa* (SAHL sah), which indicates an olive oil–based sauce of anchovies and onion.

Bisato in tecia or *alla veneziana* (bee SAH toh een TEY chah or veh neets YAH nah). This is eel, marinated in olive oil with bay leaves and vinegar, then sautéed in a frying pan, a *tecia*. This dish is known only by its name in the local Venetian dialect.

Cape sante alla veneziana (KAH pay SAHN tay ah lah veh neets YAH nah). These are scallops, sautéed simply in olive oil.

Fegato alla veneziana (feh GAH toh ah lah veh neets YAH nah). This signature dish of Veneto is calves' liver cooked with onions, sometimes drizzled with lemon juice or garnished with parsley, and invariably served with polenta.

Gamberetti. Shrimp. (See Menu Primer A to Z: *Gamberetti.*)

Garusoli (gahr oo SOH lee). These are tiny conch from the local waters, served often as part of the antipasto.

Granseole (grahn seh OH leh). The large spider crabs indigenous to the waters around Venezia are considered a delicacy. Seafood is served very simply in the area so the freshness and flavor shine through. A wedge of lemon is the reluctant accompaniment.

Nerveti (nayr VEH tee). This appetizer of tender boiled calves' feet and knuckles is marinated in raw onion, parsley, vinegar, and oil. It's a dish commonly encountered at the small bars, or *bacari,* in Venice.

Pasta e fagioli (PAH stah ay fah JOH lee). Pasta and bean soup. (See Menu Primer A to Z: *Pasta e fagioli.*)

Polenta (poh LEHN tah). Cornmeal, a staple in Veneto. (See Menu Primer A to Z: *Polenta.*)

Polenta e osei (poh LEHN tah ay OS say). Polenta served with roasted small birds, often wild game birds.

Polpeti (pol PEH tee). These are tiny, succulent octopus boiled and served warm with a dressing of oil and vinegar.

Radicchio (rah DEE kyoh). Several forms of this somewhat bitter vegetable are grown in the region, especially in the towns of Chioggia, Castelfranco, and Treviso. The radicchio of Treviso, with its elongated, purplish-red spears and white ribs, is thought to be the world's best. Although we are most accustomed to seeing this "designer" vegetable in salads, here it's usually roasted, grilled, or baked with olive oil and served as a side dish, or it is marinated with the familiar cooked onions, vinegar, pine nuts, and raisins.

Risi e bisi (REE zee ay BEE see). The Venetian dialect for *riso e piselli*, or rice with peas. It's the harbinger of springtime in Venice and perhaps the most celebrated of all the Venetian rice dishes. It's best made when the tender young peas have just been picked. A mixture of celery, onion, and sometimes garlic, parsley, and bacon is sautéed in oil and butter, then added to cooked rice. The peas are cooked separately, then added to the rice, and the dish is finished with grated Parmesan.

Risotto (ree ZOHT toh). This is a very popular *primo*, or first course, here in Veneto. The variations on the theme are truly stunning. The short-grained rice *vialone nano,* ideal for the creamy dish, is grown in the region. The flavoring agents added to the rice depend on the season as well as the location. In Venice, seafood is invariably the flavoring agent, in which case the menu will list *risotto di mare* (MAH reh) or *di pesce* (PAY shay). *Risotto nero* (NEY roh) contains cuttlefish and is colored by its mellow-tasting black ink. Further west, vegetables are often the flavoring agent, and fennel, asparagus, artichokes, beans, and fresh peas all appear at their proper time. Classic rustic risottos are made with wild game, chicken giblets, pigeon *(piccioni),* and even frogs! Risotto in Veneto is said to be be *all'onda* (ahl OHN dah), or wavelike, meaning that it should be creamy, almost liquid, not dry.

Seppie alla veneziana (SEP pyay ah lah veh neets YAH nah). This is cuttlefish cooked in their ink and served with grilled polenta.

Sfogi in saor (SFOH gee een sah OR). This is a type of tiny sole that is fried, then marinated in vinegar along with onion, pine nuts, and raisins. It is also a common treatment for small fresh sardines, or *sarde* (SAHR deh).

Tiramisù (teer ah mee SOO). An Italian dessert similar to the English trifle. Some say this treat is at its best in Veneto. (See Menu Primer A to Z: *Tiramisù.*)

Torresani allo spiedo (tor reh ZAHN ee ah loh SPYEY doh). Spit-roasted pigeon flavored with rosemary, bay leaves, and juniper berries is popular, especially inland. Look for the ever-present polenta to accompany the dish.

Tramezzini (trah me TSEE nee). These are the sandwiches of Venezia, made with small triangles of soft bread, spread with mayonnaise, and enclosing an infinite variety of meat or vegetable fillings.

MARKET BUYING TIPS

· ▉ ·

WHETHER you're strolling the streets or touring the countryside by car, one of the finest ways to hone in on the true flavor of a region is to visit the local markets. Many are outdoor markets on city streets and piazzas that set up in the morning and disappear by noon. It's there that you'll discover beautiful displays of seasonal fragrant fruits and often unusual vegetables to purchase and take along as picnic fare or to seek out on the menu that night! (By the way, this is not the place to practice your bartering skills—the prices that are posted are firm.) Specialty food shops abound and offer an array of take-out items, including cheeses, sliced meats, prepared salads, breads, and mineral water and wines. Bakeries provide sweets to complete your menu. (See Introduction.)

Many of the food items you will come across can legally be brought home. Dried foods (and that includes porcini, rice, and beans) and bottled and canned foods are fine. Cheeses must be fully cured; fresh cheeses such as mozzarella and ricotta are not allowed.

Roasted coffee *is* permitted. Don't even think about bringing in meats in any form, even the dried, cured meats like prosciutto. They will be immediately confiscated! But do check out the food shops before leaving the country, and bring home a little taste of Italy! The following will help sort out where to find the items.

Alimentari (ah lee men TAH ree). A general grocery store.

Drogheria (droh gay REE yah). These are drugstores that often sell spices (*droga* means spice as well as drug) along with packaged pantry items.

Enoteca (ayn oh TEH kah). This is a wineshop that serves as well as sells wine.

Friggitoria (free jee toh REE ah). A fry shop, found especially in Liguria, where the shops make and sell crepes made from chickpeas. (See Regional/Seasonal Specialties: Liguria: *Farinata*.)

Gastronomia (gas tron oh MEE ah). This is the Italian food store similar to the American delicatessen. It carries cold cuts and prepared foods and is a great place to shop for picnic fare.

Gelateria (jay lah teh REE ah). Ice-cream shop.

Latteria (lah teh REE ah). A shop that sells milk products.

Pasticceria (pahs tee chay REE ah). Pastry shop.

Pescheria (pey skeh REE ah). Fish market.

Rosticceria (ros tee chay REE ah). The Italian version of a fast-food take-out place, it has rotisserie-cooked poultry, roast beef, and french fries.

Salumeria (sah loo may REE yah). This is where you buy your *salumi* (cold cuts), of course. It's a great place to stop for many other picnic items like cheeses, olives, and marinated salads.

Here's a buying guide to some of Italy's special products:

Aceto balsamico (ah CHAY toh bahl SAHM ee koh). One of the truly outstanding products of the provinces of Modena and Reggio in Emilia-Romagna, true, artisanal balsamic vinegar is made from the juice of trebbiano grapes, cooked over a fire to concentrate it, then aged—sometimes for over one hundred years—in a succession of wooden barrels, made entirely of oak, chestnut, cherry, ash, or mulberry! The current rage over *balsamico* has led to many imitators from other regions, but the best is still made here. The protracted aging process takes place in attics that are exposed to the elements, both heat and cold, that further the evaporation process. The properly aged vinegar becomes rich and syrupy and tastes both sweet and sour. When purchasing balsamic vinegar to take home, look for either of the two appellations that are awarded to traditionally made products, Aceto Balsamico Tradizionale di Modena and Aceto Balsamico Tradizionale di Reggio Emilia. Other commercial vinegars made in these areas will be good as well and more reasonably priced. Ordinary balsamic vinegar can be had for as little as three to four dollars a bottle; these are no more than commercial wine vinegars flavored with caramel. At the other end of the spectrum are the finest artisan-made products, sometimes aged for several generations—the cost can be as high as fifty dollars per ounce. These incomparable, heady samples are often sipped as a liqueur or drizzled in minute quantities over finished dishes like roasted meats or frittatas, fresh fruits, especially strawberries, and even chunks of *parmigiano-reggiano*. But you can do that with the less expensive balsamic vinegars, too. Fortunately, there are many very acceptable gradations in between that are aged for perhaps five to twelve years. They are excellent, and you won't have to get a second mortgage on the house! Look for balsamic vinegars that are a deep, rich brown color. When you swirl the bottle, the syrupy liquid should coat the sides of the glass. If you have the opportunity to sample the vinegar, the aroma should be rich and intense and the taste a delicious and complex balance of sweet and sour.

Caffè. This is coffee. We call it espresso, but in Italy it's *caffè.* And although coffee beans are not grown commercially in Italy, they are roasted and ground both by local shops and by large companies like Lavazza and Illycaffè. (Their products can be found in the United States as well.) Good-quality, dark brown espresso beans are at their best when freshly ground to a fine but not powdery grind. The classic (nonelectric) inexpensive espresso-making pot, *macchinetta* (mahk ee NAHT tah), is made in a wide array of sizes and can be found in kitchen shops called *casalinghi* (kah sah LEEN gee) as well as in department-store housewares sections.

Cioccolato (chee ohk koh LAH toh). Chocolate.

- *Baci* (BAH chee). Literally, "kisses," but it's the name for delicious candies in which ground hazelnuts are covered with chocolate and topped with a whole hazelnut. The city of Perugia in Umbria is home to Perugina, a company famous for its *baci*. *Baci* make an impressive gift for those back home, although they are available, at inflated prices (and they are sometimes stale) in stores in the United States. Perugina's brightly wrapped chocolate Easter eggs have also added to the company's fame. The term *baci* also denotes a small cookie called *baci di dama* (BAH chee dee DAM ah), "lady's kisses."
- *Gianduja* (jahn DOO yah). Piemonte (in particular the city of Torino) is known for its great chocolate, but few rival *gianduja*, an inspired pair-

ing of the locally grown hazelnuts with fine imported chocolate that appears in varying forms. *Giandujotti* (jahn doo YOT tee) are the chocolates made with a filling of hazelnut cream. If you're fond of peanut butter and your diet is on hold, try *crema gianduja* (KREH mah), an addicting spread of chocolate and hazelnuts.

- In Toscana, look for fabulous liqueur-filled chocolates made by Roberto Catinari.

Confetti (kon FET tee). These are sugar-coated and multicolored almonds, similar to Jordan almonds. They're made in the region of Abruzzo and used in celebrations all over Italy, including weddings, anniversaries, birthdays, and graduations. Each color denotes a different year for birthdays and anniversaries or relates to various areas such as medicine, law, or business.

Farro (FAR roh). Called "emmer" in English, this delicious, barleylike grain is made into hearty soups or stone-ground and combined with whole-wheat flour to make rustic pastas such as *manfrigoli* in Umbria. If you sample the soups or pastas and fall in love, you can find packages of the whole grain as well as the flour in many food shops, especially in Umbria and Marche. They are easily transportable, and there is no problem bringing grains and flours into the United States—just be sure to declare them.

Fave di morte (FAH vay dee MAWR teh). Literally "fava beans of the dead," these cookies are shaped like fava beans, an ancient emblem of the dead in both Italy and Greece. These "dead men's cookies" are eaten to honor the dead on All Souls' Day. A regional difference includes grappa in the Venetian version. They are made of ground almonds, sugar, flour, and usually pine nuts. Additional flavorings such as grappa or cinnamon may be added.

Fichi (FEE kee). Fresh figs of outstanding quality are grown in the region of Abruzzo. Definitely worth trying!

Formaggi (for MAHD jee). Cheeses. To bring cheese back to the United States, it must be fully cured (a minimum of ninety days), so fresh cheeses like ricotta and mozzarella must be eaten while you are there—the perfect excuse for tasting as many as possible during your stay! But many of the truly great cheeses of Italy like *parmigiano-reggiano*, pecorino, and fontina can be brought home. You might see if the shop will shrink-wrap your selections—this will help keep them fresh, and they will be less likely to "perfume" the rest of your luggage! (See Menu Primer A to Z: *Formaggio*.)

The regional cheeses of Italy actually outnumber those of France. Read the section of Regional/Seasonal Specialties on the regions you are visiting for some of the not-to-be missed varieties. A few of the most exceptional cheeses include the following:

- *Fontina* (fon TEE nah). The milky-tasting, buttery-flavored, easily melting cheese of Valle d'Aosta and one of Italy's most outstanding dairy products. Very little of it is exported. (In American markets, we usually get the red-rinded Scandinavian fontina. The Italian fontina has a brown rind.) Most is eaten when it's quite young, especially in *fonduta,* the Italian version of fondue. A canned version of this specialty, also called *fonduta,* is available in stores. (See Menu Primer A to Z: *Fontina* and Regional/Seasonal Specialties: Piemonte: *Fonduta con tartufo* and Valle d'Aosta: Introduction.)

- *Gorgonzola* (gor gon ZOH lah). This rich, creamy, and pungent blue Italian cheese has been produced just outside Milano in Lombardia and in Piemonte since the eighth century. Fair warning! Be sure to wrap this aromatic cheese well if you're taking it along on a picnic or back to the room! (See Menu Primer A to Z: *Gorgonzola* and Regional/Seasonal Specialties: Lombardia: Introduction.)

- *Grana* (GRAH nah) or *grana padana* (GRAH nah pah DAH nah). Another very good grating cheese, produced primarily in Lombardia. Although similar to *parmigiano-reggiano,* it will be somewhat less expensive since it is made under slightly less stringent conditions and is not as revered by aficionados. (See Menu Primer A to Z: *Grana.*)

- *Mascarpone* (mahs kahr POH nay). The soft and creamy cheese from Emilia-Romagna has many ardent fans, especially those who love tiramisù, in which it's an essential ingredient. Look for mascarpone in savory dishes as well as desserts. This is a cheese you'll want to sample here, as it can't be transported home. (See Menu Primer A to Z: *Mascarpone* and *Tiramisù*.)

• *Mozzarella* (motz tzah REHL lah). If the opportunity arises, be sure to taste the delicious cheese made from rich buffalo milk, *di bufala* (BOO fah lah), made mostly in the region of Campania. Both the texture and flavor are very different from most stateside mozzarellas. Some mozzarella is made from a combination of buffalo's and cow's milk. The cow's milk variety, *mozzarella fior di latte* (FYOR dee LAT tay), is easier to find and also deserves tasting. This is a fresh cheese, one you won't be allowed to bring back into the United States, so plan accordingly. (See Menu Primer A to Z: *Insalata caprese* and *Mozzarella*, Comfort Foods: Eggplant Parmesan, Pasta and Pizza, and Regional/Seasonal Specialties: Campania: Introduction, *Melanzane alla mozzarella*, and *Mozzarella in carrozza*.)

• *Parmigiano-reggiano* (pahr mee JAH noh reh JAHN oh). This world-class cheese of Emilia-Romagna can be purchased and brought home with you. The cost in the United States is about twelve to fifteen dollars per pound, but it can be found for less in food shops in Italy. Look for the PARMIGIANO-REGGIANO perforated lettering on the surface, as well as the date stamped there. The cheese should be aged for two years, although longer aging produces a more complex product and commands higher prices. If kept tightly wrapped, the cheese stays fresh in the refrigerator for at least a couple of months. When sliced, it has light-colored flecks throughout. This is not mold but bits of protein that add to the cheese's delightful texture. Parmesan should be grated just before serving. (Proper cheese graters called *grattugia* [grah TOO jah] can be found in Italian kitchen shops.) (See Menu Primer A to Z: *Carpaccio* and *Parmigiano-reggiano*, Comfort Foods: Eggplant Parmesan and Veal, and Regional/Seasonal Specialties: Calabria: *Parmigiano di melanzane* and Emilia-Romagna: Introduction.)

• *Pecorino* (peh koh REE noh). Sheep's milk cheese can be either fresh, in which case it's mild, or aged, when the taste becomes decidedly more distinct and the texture hardens to the point where the cheese is used for grating. Innumerable variations are found, mostly in the southern regions, especially Lazio and Sardegna, where grazing land for cattle is sparse and sheep herding is more viable. It's often called *pecorino romano,* or *stagionato* (stah jo NAH toh), "of the season." A cheese made in the spring, when the sheep feed on tender young grass, will differ from one made from milk gathered later in the summer. Much pecorino is made on the island of Sardegna. The Lazio cheese has a slight green cast, a consequence of the aging in tufa, or limestone, caves. The Sardinian cheese is whiter. There are so many variations in flavor that you should try to sample a little before buying. The aged pecorino may be brought home. If it's very well wrapped, it will keep for at least a month. (See Menu Primer A to Z: *Pecorino*, Regional/Seasonal Specialties: Abruzzo: *Formaggio di pecora*, Lazio: Introduction, and Sardegna: Introduction.)

- *Ricotta* (ree KOHT tah). The soft, mild-flavored fresh cheese made from whey is familiar to most Americans. Most regions make a version of this cheese that's well worth sampling. The ricotta of Lazio, *ricotta romana*, is exceptional, and some are quite unusual, such as *ricotta affumicata*, the smoked ricotta from the region of Friuli–Venezia Giulia.

- *Squaquerone* (skwah kweh ROH neh). This is a delicious fresh, soft, almost liquid cheese from Emilia-Romagna. Take some on your picnic— along with plenty of napkins!

- *Taleggio* (tah LEG gyoh). It's from Lombardia, but you should be able to find this smooth and luscious cow's milk cheese in most northern regions. Try it if you can. It's too good to miss!

Funghi (FOON ghee). Mushrooms, especially the huge fresh and meaty porcini (por CHEE nee), are highly prized in Italy for their intense flavor and woodsy aroma. They're served in soups, salads, and pastas and even appear as the main event in the vegetable course, or *contorno*. Dried porcini are used extensively as well, where they serve more as a flavoring agent. They are usually sold in cellophane packages in Italy, at a lower price than you'll find them back home. If you decide to purchase some, be sure the package says PORCINI (otherwise they may be another type of wild mushroom), and look for large pieces rather than crumbled bits.

Grappa (GRAHP pah). This "high-octane" digestif, made from the grape skins and pits that remain after the wine-making process, was traditionally akin to moonshine. But in recent years, both the art and science of grappa making have reached new heights, and marketing practices have been notable. Today's fine products packaged in their magnificent glass bottles make such exceptional take-home gifts that you may not want to give them away! *Grappa monovitigno* (mon oh vee TEE nyoh) is distilled from a single grape variety. Some of the best grappas are made in the northeastern region of Friuli–Venezia Giulia, but the regions of Emilia-Romagna, Piemonte, Toscana, Trentino–Alto Adige, and Umbria all produce good-quality grappa. (See Menu Primer A to Z: *Grappa* and Beverages A to Z: *Digestivi: Grappa.*)

Lenticchie (len TEE kee ay). Lentils. The Umbrian lentils, touted as the finest in Italy, are smaller than most. If lentils are your passion, you can buy them in many Umbrian food shops and bring them home. (See Menu Primer A to Z: *Lenticchie.*)

Marsala (mahr SAHL lah). This exquisite fortified wine is produced in Sicilia, where it is made sweet (*dolce*), semidry (*semisecco*), and dry (*secco*). Used in both sweet and savory dishes, it's available back in the United States, but you'll find a wider variety of styles and producers in Italy. (See Menu Primer A to Z: *Zabaione*, Comfort Foods: Veal, and Regional/Seasonal Specialties: Lombardia: Introduction and *Piccata al marsala* and Sicilia: Introduction.)

Olio d'oliva (OL yoh d'oh LEE vah). Olive oil and Italy are nearly synonymous in our minds and rightly so. But as in wines, the olive oils of Italy are so varied that it's best to taste the oils of the different regions in order to decide on your favorites. The highest grade is extra virgin; it denotes the first pressing of the olives, which yields the oil with the lowest acidity. Oils can be filtered or not (simply a matter of preference), and the taste will be most pronounced (some say harsh) when the oil is freshly pressed; this is considered a positive attribute by aficionados. Some oils are marked with vintage dates, and it's actually best to use the oil within eighteen months or so. The peppery-tasting extra virgin olive oil of Toscana is thought by many to be the best, but let your own taste buds be your guide. The oils of Umbria and Lazio are gutsier, while those of Liguria are lighter and more delicate. Italian oils (carefully packed!) make terrific take-home gifts. Be sure to store your treasure in a cool, dry, and dark place. (See Menu Primer A to Z: *Olio d'oliva*.)

Pane (PAH nay). Breads come in every conceivable shape, size, and texture in Italy. In Toscana, bread is mostly made without salt to accompany the highly flavored, sometimes salty *cucina* properly. Piemonte makes the finest breadsticks, *grissini*. Other northern regions influenced by Austria and Germany make black or rye breads. The focaccia of Liguria is legendary. The crisp, crackerlike bread of Sardegna, *pane carasau*, is outstanding. Wherever your travels lead you, you'll want to sample the local breads and bring them along on picnics or for snacks.

Panettone (pah net TOH neh). This rich, yeasty cake with a briochelike texture is originally from Milano, where it appears especially at Christmas. But it's become so popular that bakers now bake *panettone* at other times, too. It's filled with raisins and candied fruit and makes a nice change from the season's fruitcake that's so common in the United States. (See Menu Primer A to Z: *Panettone* and Regional/Seasonal Specialties: Lombardia: Introduction.)

Pasta (PAH stah). Pastas are of two persuasions: fresh and dry. If you are lucky enough to have a kitchen in which to experiment while on your trip, you can purchase prepared pastas, such as the famous tortellini in Emilia-Romagna, and enjoy. Otherwise, the dry pastas are your focus. Since you can buy pastas—both domestic and imported—at home, you may hesitate to take up valuable luggage space with it. But if you care to investigate, there are some exceptional high-quality pastas produced by small, artisanal companies made "the old-fashioned way" with bronze plates (instead of Teflon ones) to extrude the pasta. This creates pasta with a rougher surface, which tends to attract and hold the sauce instead of letting it slip off. These companies allow a longer drying period, which is also beneficial. The pastas of Abruzzo, such as brand names *Del Verde* and *De Cecco,* are said to be superior, in part because of the region's excellent water. (See Menu Primer A to Z: *Pasta* and Comfort Foods: Pasta.)

Riso (REE zoh). Rice. If you've fallen in love with risotto (ree ZOHT toh), you might want to bring back some of the special rices used in cooking this culinary treat. Arborio, the rice most widely used in the United States for risotto, is generally available at home in well-stocked grocery stores and specialty food shops. There are, however, some other short-grained rices that are venerated by connoisseurs and difficult to find outside Italy. One of the most highly prized is *carnaroli,* which is grown in the northern regions. In Veneto, where they prefer their risotto a little more liquid in texture, the favorite is their regionally produced *Vialone nano.* Back home, these are pretty pricey—from three to seven dollars per pound—so they might be worth tucking into your bag. (See Menu Primer A to Z: *Risotto* and Regional/Seasonal Specialties: Lombardia: Introduction and *Risotto alla milanese,* Piemonte: *Panissa,* and Veneto: Introduction and *Risotto.*)

Salumi (sah LOO mee). This is an all-encompassing term for cured meats such as prosciutto and salami. Traditionally, most of the meat consumed by the poor was in the form of preserved meats, especially pork, in *salumi,* prosciutto, and *salsiccie* (sausage). Regional variations in the curing process, the locally available flavoring agents, and the varying climates have created delicious nuances in the products, and if you're planning a picnic or want to stock your room or touring car with some tasty snacks, check out the local salumeria or try the *alimentari,* or general grocery store, where they sell all kinds of cold cuts and *salumi* like *prosciutto cotto* (cooked ham) and *prosciutto crudo* (salted and air-cured ham). You should be able to buy a few slices of meats, along with other items for your lunch or snack, such as cheeses, olives, salads, and mineral water.

As you tour the regions, try to sample the local specialties. In Friuli–Venezia Giulia, you'll find the incredible *prosciutto crudo di San Daniele,* and try the brine- and smoke-cured *Speck* in Trentino–Alto Adige. In Veneto, cold cuts made with wild game, *Salumi di cacciagione,* are worth seeking out. In Emilia-Romagna, the list seems endless, but don't miss the world-famous *prosciutto di Parma* and mortadella. Toscana makes a variety of salami called *soppressata,* and versions of this are also made in the southern regions. Toscana's fennel-spiked pork sausage, *finocchiona,* and *prosciutto di cinghiale,* ham made from wild boar, are additional treats. *Finocchiella* (fee nok KYEL lah) is the name for the pork sausage of Umbria that's flavored with fennel seeds, and while you're in the neighborhood, don't miss Umbria's *prosciutto di Norcia*. The pork butchers of the town of Norcia are respected throughout the country for their excellent *salumi*. The spiced sausage of Basilicata, *lucanica*, is exceptional, and if you're a fan of blood sausage, the *soppressata* is interesting as well. While in Umbria and Calabria, you'll no doubt run into the spicy *capocollo*. By the way, enjoy these treats while you can, but don't plan on taking them home in your suitcase. U.S. Customs will not allow you to bring in any meats. For many years, Italian prosciutto was banned altogether from the United States, but now official importers can bring it in, and vendors sell it for about twenty-four dollars per pound. (See Menu Primer A to Z: *Capocollo*, *Cotechino*, *Prosciutto*, *Salumi*, and *Soppressata* and Regional/Seasonal Specialties: Emilia-Romagna: *Coppa*, *Cotechino*, *Culatello*, and *Mortadella*, Friuli–Venezia Giulia: *Musett*, Lombardia: *Bresaola*, and Puglia: Introduction.)

Tartufi (tar TOOF ee). Two distinct type of truffles are found in Italy, the black, *neri* (NAY ree) truffle and the highly prized white truffles, *tartufo bianco* (tar TOOF oh be AHN koh). The wooded mountains, hills, and valleys of Umbria boast an abundance of black truffles, an ingredient that appears on local menus from December through May. In the past, the truffles were routed out by enormous pigs, who relished the taste of the delicacy, but today highly trained dogs are often used to sniff out the truffles, as they can be rewarded with some other treat and the truffle hunter doesn't have to battle a large, overwrought pig for the "black gold." Black truffles come canned or preserved as creams, pastes, and in olive oil, so you can transport the flavor home with you. The better ones, harvested during the fall months, are marked PREGIATI and will be more costly than those dug up in spring *(scorzoni).*

Even more highly prized than black truffles are white truffles, which are found mainly in the provinces of Alba and Asti in Piemonte but also in Lombardia, and Emilia-Romagna. The height of the white truffle season is late October and November and December, and their presence on the menu is heralded by the intense aroma that permeates the room. The white truffle is never cooked (as opposed to the black truffle) but is shaved raw onto risottos, pastas, and salads. The commercial truffle market is unlike any other—much secrecy, a total lack of regulations, and astronomical prices abound (as much as two hundred dollars per ounce), which makes buying fresh white truffles challenging, to say the least. Truffles begin to deteriorate quickly once they are harvested, so they should be used as soon as possible. Fresh truffles are allowed into the United States as long as the soil has been carefully removed. But white truffle oil, as well as a wide range of other truffle-scented products, make terrific take-home gifts. (See Menu Primer A to Z: *Tartufi,* Regional/

Seasonal Specialties: Piemonte: *Fonduta con tartufo* and *Tartufi*, and Umbria: *Tartufi*.)

Torrone (tor ROH nay). Nougat. The regional variations of this delicious candy reflect the local produce. The wonderful hazelnuts of Piemonte are toasted, then join forces with honey, sugar, and egg whites. Next, the mixture is cooked for several hours. In Calabria, you might find *torrone* with candied orange and ground almonds and dipped in chocolate. Sicily often includes almonds and sesame seeds in its *torrone*. In Abruzzo, the confection is flavored with almonds, their excellent dried figs, or chocolate. These delicacies make great take-home gifts—they're sturdy and easy to pack.

Torta al testo (TOR tah ahl TEYS toh). Unleavened flatbread from Umbria, cooked on flat stones. Shop early in the day, and take one along in the picnic basket.

USEFUL WORDS
QUICK REFERENCE GUIDE

· ■ ·

Bill. *Il Conto* (EEL KON toh). The bill, please!—*Il Conto, per favore* (EEL KON toh, PEYR fah VO reh).

Bottle. *Bottiglia* (bot TEEL yah).

Bottle opener. *Apribottiglia* (ah pree bot TEEL yah).

Bread. *Pane* (PAH nay).

Breadsticks. *Grissini* (gree SEE nee).

Breakfast. *Colazione* (kohl ah tzee OH nay). The upper class may refer to it as *prima colazione* or *picolo colazione*.

Closed. *Chiuso* (KYOO soh). Days closed. *Giorno di chiusura* (JOR noh dee KYOO soo rah). All restaurants are closed one or two days a week. Fish markets and restaurants are generally closed Monday since the fishermen take Sunday off.

Cold. *Freddo* (FRED doh).

Corkscrew. *Cavatappi* (kah vah TAHP pee).

Cover charge. *Coperto* (koh PAIR toh).

Cup. *Tazza* (TAT tzah).

Dinner. *Cena* (CHEY nah). Also known as *pranzo* (PRAHN tsoh) to the upper class.

Flatware. *Posate* (paw SAH teh).

Fork. *Forchetta* (for KAYT tah).

Glass. *Bicchiere* (beek YEH ray).

Hot. *Caldo* (KAL doh).

Ice. *Ghiaccio* (GYAHT choh).

Knife. *Coltello* (kohl TEL loh).

Lunch. *Pranzo* (PRAHN tsoh) is the term used by the average Italian. The upper class might use the term *colazione* (kohl ah tzee OH nay).

Medium. *Al punto* (POON toh). Refers to how well cooked you want your food.

Medium rare. *Poco cotta* (POH koh KOT tah).

Menu. *Lista* (LEE stah).

Milk. *Latte* (LAHT teh).

Mustard. *Senape* (say NAH pay).

Napkin. *Tovagliolo* (toh val YOH loh) or *Salvietta* (sahl VYET tah).

Nonalcoholic beverages. *Analcolico* (ahn ahl KOHL ee koh).

Pardon me. *Scusi* (SCOO zee).

Plate. *Piatto* (PYAHT toh).

Rare. *Al sangue* (SAN gway).

Reservation. *Prenotazione* (preyn oh tah TSYOH nay).

Restroom. *Gabinetto* (gah bee NET toh).

Salt and pepper. *Sale e pepe* (SAH leh ay PEY peh).

Service charge. *Servizio* (seyr VEE tzee oh).

Snack. *Merenda* (mey REN dah).

Spoon. *Cucchiaio* (kook KYAH yoh).

Store or shop. *Bottega* (bot TEY gah).

Sugar. *Zucchero* (TSOOK kay roh).

Table. *Tavola* (TAH vo lah).

Tip. *Mancia* (MAHN chah).

Waiter. *Signore* (seen YO reh). This is the proper term to be used when addressing the waiter.

Waitress. *Signorina* or *Signora* (seen yo REE nah or seen YO rah). *Signora* is the term to use if she is somewhat older or if she is wearing a wedding ring.

Water. *Acqua* (AH kwah). Mineral water is *acqua minerale* (mee neh RAH lay). It comes either *gassata* (gahs SAH tah), or *con gas* (with carbonation), or *naturale* (nah too RAH leh) (without bubbles). Italian tap water is safe to drink unless you see a sign saying *acqua non potabile* (po tah BEE leh). (See Beverages A to Z: *Acqua minerale*.)

Well done. *Cotta bene* (KOT tah BAY nay).

NOTES

NOTES

NOTES

NOTES

NOTES

NOTES

NOTES

NOTES

_____

_____

_____

_____

_____

_____

_____

_____

_____

_____

_____

_____

_____

_____